Earle Sieveling's
New York Cuisine

Earle Sieveling's
New York Cuisine

McGraw-Hill Book Company
New York   St. Louis   San Francisco   Auckland   Bogotá
Guatemala   Hamburg   Johannesburg   Lisbon   London   Madrid
Mexico   Montreal   New Delhi   Panama   Paris   San Juan
São Paulo   Singapore   Sydney   Tokyo   Toronto

Copyright © 1985 by Earle Sieveling

All rights reserved. Printed in the United States of America. Except as permitted under the Copyright Act of 1976, no part of this publication may be reproduced or distributed in any form or by any means, or stored in a data base or retrieval system, without the written permission of the publisher.

Photography by David Cook
Selected flower designs by Arthur Ray
Concept by Maud Ann Cauley
Book design by Barbara M. Marks

1 2 3 4 5 6 7 8 9 D O C D O C 8 7 6 5 4

ISBN 0-07-057295-X

LIBRARY OF CONGRESS CATALOGING IN PUBLICATION DATA

Sieveling, Earle.
  Earle Sieveling's New York cuisine.

  Includes index.
  1. Cookery, American—New York (State) 2. Cookery, International. 3. New York (N.Y.)—Social life and customs. I. Title. II. Title: New York cuisine.
TX715.S579   1985   641.5   84-7133
ISBN 0-07-057295-X

Give a man a fish and
you feed him for a day —
teach a man to fish and
you feed him for a lifetime.

Thank you "Mr. B"

Acknowledgments

I wish to thank Tom Dembofsky, Ken Stuart, PJ Haduch, Barbara Kastner, Roberta Rezk, David Cook, Rosemary Bennett, Arthur Ray, Robert Kasanof, Howard Heiss, Stephanie L. White, and Steven Chernesky.

Author's Note

Throughout the recipes in this book you will see kosher salt specified. Both kosher and natural sea salt contain fewer chemicals than regular salt, and therefore produce a more natural result.

From time to time I indicate the use of a name-brand product. While substitutions can be made, that product has been listed because of its qualities, and replacing it will somewhat change the final result.

Contents

Crown of Shrimp

Preface
page xix

Introduction
page xxiii

Chapter I

Sensitivity
...understanding the elements
page 1

Fifth Avenue Oysters
Asparagus Maltaise
Artichoke Ragoût
Chicken with Butter and Tarragon under the Skin
Accompanied by Baby Carrots and Leeks
Spinach Soup
Terrine of Veal
Lobster Bisque
Rack of Lamb with Rosemary and Garlic
Ragoût of Lobster on a Mound of Lingue di Passero

Chapter II

Selection
...the market speaks

page 17

Wild Mushroom Soup
Poached Pears
Sparrows' Tongues (Linguine) with Avocado and Salsa
Virginia Oak Mushrooms with Shallots
Filets of Striped Bass with Sweet Peppers, Lime, and Cream
Double-Baked Potato and Leek Soufflé
Filets of Sole with Cucumber, Crème Fraîche, and Fresh Mint
Torta
Mussel Soup
Lobster, Shrimp, Scallops, and Leeks
Wild Rice with Apricots and Hazelnuts
Seafood Lasagne

Chapter III

Tonic Chord
...rediscovering the essence

page 39

Seafood Ravioli
Pizza Crust
Raspberry Fruit Tarts with Chocolate
Snails in Garlic Cream
Parboiled Sautéed Potatoes
Herb Toast
Pizza Turnovers
Bouillabaisse

Chapter IV

Dialogue
...the nature of things

page 59

Filet of Beef with Oriental Black Beans and Sweet Peppers
Frozen Espresso with Chocolate Curls and Cream
Calves' Liver with Root Vegetables
Potato Salad with Garlic, Grana, and Double-Smoked Bacon
Cold Pork Salad with Cucumbers and Sesame Noodles
Asparagus, Westphalian Ham, and Pasta with Chèvre Sauce
Butter Cream Cake
Wild Rice Salad
Scrambled Eggs on Gravlax
Stuffed Potatoes
Red Snapper in an Aromatic Broth
with Vegetables and Ginger Hollandaise

Chapter V

Heightening
...bringing food up to taste

page 79

Shoulder of Pork with Prosciutto and Green Peppercorns
Snow Peas with Fresh Mint and Shallots
Shell Steak with Three Pepppers
Steak Tartare
Pork Curry with Root Vegetables
Duck Livers with Sherry Wine Vinegar
Belgian Carrots in Rosemary Butter
Red Snapper in Red Wine Sauce
Veal Chops with Sun-Dried Tomatoes and Fontina Cheese

Chapter VI
Texture
...the final result

page 95

Odile Chocolate Cake
Smoked Tuna with White Beans
Sabayon au Poire
Brie Italienne
Sautéed Breast of Duck with Confit of Duck
Custard
Food Processor Ice Creams
Food Processor Sorbet
Cucumber Salad
Banana Mousse Pie
Carpaccio
Salmon Mousseline
Quenelles

Chapter VII
Heat
...and its application

page 119

Vegetable Curry with Hot Tortilla Chips
Standing Rib Roast
Baked Spinach
Beignets
Shrimp and Scallops on Linguine
(High Heat Method)
Stuffed Leg of Lamb
Potato Salad with Jalapeños and Sweet Red Peppers

Turnips en Papillote
Tarte Tatin
Egg-Roll Satchels
Haricots Verts with Bay Scallops and Sherry Wine Vinegar
Pan-Broiled Swordfish with Lemon-Basil Vinaigrette
Chaud-Froid Brioches
Steak Putanesca

Chapter VIII

Composition
...color, balance, form

page 143

Crown of Shrimp
Fruit Soup
Filet of Sole with Beurre Blanc and Steamed Spinach
Sour Cherry Compote
Braised Loin of Pork with Cranberries, Sage, and Tangerines
Chestnut Cream with Chocolate Shavings (Monte Bianco de Maronne)
Medallions of Veal with Three Mushrooms
Soft-Shell Crabs in Beurre Blanc with Swirls of Caviar

Chapter IX

Security Blanket
...food for the soul

page 157

Chicken with Garlic, Sealed in a Crust
Cornbread Stuffing
Clam Soup

Corn Relish
Putanesca Sauce
Chicken Pot Pie
Potatoes au Gratin
Black Bean and Madeira Soup
Braised Cabbage
Maple Walnut Pie
Polenta
Chicken Fried in the Southern Style
Sausage Toasts with Garlic Cream
Potato and Leek Soup
Linguiça and Kale Soup

Chapter X

Ambiance
...all and everything

page 177

Scallop Bisque with Seafood Sausage
Risotto with White Truffles
Oysters in Garlic Cream with Shallots
Charcuterie Platter
Capelli d'Angeli with Salmon and Caviar
Seafood Sausage
Lace Tulip Cookies
Polenta with Sausage, Chicken, and Tomato Sauce
Lobster Toast
Pheasant with a Compote of Pineapple Quince, Artichoke Hearts, and Chestnuts
Coulibiac

Chapter XI
Basic Preparations
...simple, but not easy

page 199

Fish Fumet
Fish Stock without Fish
Beef-Veal Stock
Chicken Stock
Glace de Viande
Rémoulade Sauce
Salsa
Velouté
Hollandaise Sauce
Mayonnaise
Beurre Blanc
Tomato Sauce
Brioche Dough
Pastry Dough
Crêpes
Cornbread
Poaching
Fresh Pasta
Wild Rice
Spinach
Garlic Purée
Garlic Croûtons
Crème Fraîche
Meringue

Glossary
page 221

Index
page 223

Preface

I have written this book to free the person in the kitchen. I have never invented or created, but rather assembled and devised. For those who do not know, and perhaps for some of those that do, I have logged some little tricks, or *petits trucs* as they say in French. Perhaps they will make it easier, or rivet your attention at a moment crucial to the success of the recipe.

I have tried to hone the senses—to appreciate the beauty of splitting an onion and looking into its heart or feel the joy of opening the oven to a gloriously risen soufflé.

The combinations here may be new to you, and of course I hope they are interesting. But the techniques are age-old, as are several of the classic approaches to certain recipes.

Go, experiment, and enjoy the successes—and the failures! From our failures we learn—an old adage that a teacher of mine voiced often. It gave me courage, time and again. As they say, "What are they going to do, hit you?"

Cook and enjoy.

My joy at this point is in passing on or, more important, communicating the thrill of preparing beautiful and delicious food and hopefully how to do it.

Food is taste, and the chemical reactions which alter it. Each of the chapters in this book is designed to reacquaint you with the basic reasons for the different techniques used in cooking. Therefore, technical terms such as "apply heat" make you rethink the actual, physical action taking place. A chef is aware that cooking is a progressive process. It is not something that you start at the beginning and taste at the very end. Different chemical reactions occur during each step. A chef very frequently tastes time and again, not just with the addition of an ingredient, but when the addition or the application of heat or cold may change the taste. When you add wine to a sauce, it changes the taste. However, when you have simmered it and taste it again, you begin to understand the reaction that takes place—even though no additional ingredients have been added, only heat.

When you cook and prepare food, you are interacting with it, and I continuously stress the importance of being involved in the process. My grandmother, when asked how long something should be cooked, would answer, "Until it is done." When asked, "Well, when is it done?" she would answer, "When it is cooked." This demonstrates a thorough understanding of this principle. Approximate cooking times are certainly noted in this book, as are approximate measurements, all of which have been thoroughly tested. But each piece of fish or meat is different—because of what it has eaten, its density, and when it was killed. You can never depend solely on timings or measurements. You must be a part of the process!

Most of the recipes in this book are not very demanding. Some that appear to be simple, such as beurre blanc, are really the most complex. Don't walk away from the pan on a prolonged basis. Recognize those times when your involvement is necessary. Understand the principles and reasons why. This is the difference between a preparation that is perfect and fine and one that is only passable, or fails completely.

New York Cuisine is truly American in perspective. It is developed from the melting pot that is New York City itself, where I have the opportunity to pick and glean and choose—to add and subtract—ingredients, tastes, colors, and textures from many cuisines. One filet of sole recipe combines a French beurre blanc with steamed spinach, which is more Oriental in technique. The underlying element in all of this is my desire for simplicity, which is elegance . . . and for a complete lack of pretense in food.

Artur Rubinstein once told some of his friends that he was sure he would have been a much better technician if he had spent more hours of his days practicing and fewer on the social circuit. However, he felt that those hours he spent locked in with the piano would not have made him nearly as great a pianist. He credited his ability to communicate his *joie de vivre* in his music to his exposure to life.

I believe that all art interrelates. Many, if not most, of my concepts are gleaned not only from my experience with food but also from my experiences as a part of the New York City Ballet and from my interaction with world-class artists such as Balanchine and Stravinsky. Experiencing their sensitivity, their intense drive to create simply and beautifully, and their approach to composition, texture, and movement, has served as the groundwork for my own point of view.

I've often thought cooking is like choreography. When first learning a step, you have to master it. Once it's mastered, you can speed up. The same holds true with basic cooking preparations. As you become more familiar and more confident with the principles that are involved, they become second nature to you and you can move on.

Introduction

New York Cuisine is the intentional intermingling of ingredients and techniques from all over the world, with the only caveat being that the result must be delicious. It is the outgrowth of the abundance of fresh foods from all countries readily available in New York, combined with influences from the myriad cultures represented in this city. This cross-pollination allows the emergence of unique dishes, unrestricted by a single culinary tradition.

An art form cannot be taught—it can only be unfolded. *New York Cuisine* is clean, pure, and truthful to the ingredients. Cooking is an exposed art, like dance and opera. Less than perfect performances are immediately apparent to the viewer. *New York Cuisine*'s emphasis is on drawing from the natural qualities of the ingredients, while at the same time enhancing them. Thus there is little margin for error. *New York Cuisine* strives to bring out the opalescence of a sauce and is not afraid to allow a new reality to emerge from the ingredients. The combination of ingredients has a new significance, one that becomes more than the individual parts. This not only stems from the combination of the tastes but is dependent on the relationships of color, texture, size, and balance. *New York Cuisine* is a natural outgrowth of an artist's perception of what foods can be combined, in the only place in the world where on a daily basis the freshest ingredients are available. Additionally, I strive to make sure that the reader becomes mindful of what substitutions may be appropriate in a dish. If when you arrive at the market and a particular ingredient is not there, it should not send you running home in panic because the recipe cannot be prepared.

One of the basic principles of *New York Cuisine* is the concept of returning to the "tonic chord," that which originally spawned that type of dish. When preparing a pizza, the tonic chord is the crust upon which all the other elements are built. Frequently, cooks believe that the most important element is the sauce, or the cheese, or the herbs. They lose sight of what the pizza truly is. The basic element is the crust, and to solve all of the problems involved in preparing the proper crust—with lightness, texture, and an identity of its own—is paramount. It is not just something that serves as an edible plate for the rest of the ingredients. With that perfect crust, all the variations and many more can then be devised.

While there are established techniques and certain basic rules that can be learned, once they are learned they can also be broken, *when* there is a reason for doing so.

George Balanchine had a wonderful recipe for making pickles:

> "First, take clean jar and put in cucombers,
> Then put in veenegar,
> Deel,
> Then put in more cucombers,
> More deel,
> Then put in more cucombers,
> Cover with salty vater,
> Store two veeks—and vat do you have?
> ... PEEKLES!"

While that is not a very elucidating recipe, to a large extent it is the best way to explain making pickles. The major emphasis in this book will be on opening your eyes to the idea that the preparation of fine food can never be rigid. It changes, it evolves, and when it becomes static, it loses its vital qualities.

The word "fine" is very important. There is a major difference between "fine" and "extraordinary." While "extraordinary" may at first glance appear to be more than, "fine" implies a subtlety and a balance. It is daytime diamonds or a mink-lined raincoat: they never shout out the fact that they are diamonds or mink. They are elements that need to be there. Over the years we have become so accustomed to drinking prepared orange juice instead of fresh that a child often finds the taste of fresh orange juice strange. Well aged meat is almost nonexistent in people's taste experience today, and yet it is quite an important element in making a dish utterly delicious.

Sensitivity and awareness need to be awakened. Each rack of lamb, each piece of beef, even from the same butcher, will have a different water content, depending upon the season and the feed it has been given. This does affect cooking times, so I encourage the reader to become sensitized to the texture and look of doneness.

It is my desire to induce an overall evocation of the senses, through image rather than specific teachings, to make sure that you are aware of the total effect necessary to, and created by, fine food.

Food has the ability to communicate on two different levels, the theoretical and the sensual. Over the past twenty years, I have developed concepts that have ultimately led to the formation of a vision of what I believe food as an art form should be. My interest in food began as a child, when I lived in the Boston area, where there is an abundance of wonderful fresh seafood. It was there that I also began my dance career. While with a regional company in Boston, George Balanchine invited me to join the New York City Ballet. This exposed me to new cultures, their food preparations, and the way food becomes an art form through its preparation and service.

When I moved to New York City in the early 1960s, I had to function on the small *corps de ballet* wage of $87 a week. In order to survive, I started to develop what had been merely a hobby into a study. This pursuit was soon aided by traveling the world with the New York City Ballet and being exposed to magnificent banquets and receptions, such as those given by Princess Grace and Prince Rainier, as well as the simple yet elegant meals served in the European railroad stations. For an American, it is almost impossible to believe the attention to detail and the fineness of the food in some of those European railroad restaurants. To Europeans, there is a passionate interrelationship between food and life. It is an artistic statement, an all-encompassing emotion. When I retired from City Ballet and became a professional chef, I felt my artistic development continued, but in a new medium.

Historically, countries have developed a cuisine based upon the ingredients that are available within a region, or that are available at a particular time of the year. In some instances, a cuisine was developed to mask the limitations of certain ingredients. Many of the heavy sauces of French cuisine and the curries of India were invented to cover up inexpensive cuts of meat, or meat that had basically gone by. Over the past several years, individual cuisines have evolved as an outgrowth of these culinary traditions.

I find it most distressing when people talk about Nouvelle Cuisine as though it were invented recently. In fact, Monsieur Fernand Point originated the concept in the 1930s, and it continued to develop under three-star chefs like Paul Bocuse and Pierre and Jean Troisgros. Many unknowing chefs imitate what they perceive to be the concepts of Nouvelle Cuisine. When a building designed by architect Mies van der Rohe is copied, it has only the semblance of a Mies van der Rohe creation, without the essence of his design intent. Today's Nouvelle Cuisine is frequently only an imitation of the original—it has lost its raison d'être and vitality. In truth, Nouvelle Cuisine is far from tasteless, light, or bland.

Until the advent of the jet age, a chef has been limited by the seasonality of certain ingredients. Unless one was the Empress of China, who sent a rotating stream of runners 700 miles to maintain her constant supply of fresh lichee nuts throughout the year, a great variety of foods have not been available to a cook, regardless of cost. The average cook in America, I believe, has time limitations and cannot afford to spend an entire day shopping for ingredients from place to place. What is truly wonderful about New York and many other major metropolitan areas today is they have an abundance of fine fresh ingredients from all over the world, flown in daily. Living in New York, it is possible for me to prepare a dinner of fish that was caught the day before in the streams of France, a foie gras from Hungary, truffles and morels from Italy, Westphalian ham from Germany, spinach from the San Joaquin Valley in California, butter from Normandy, strawberries from Australia, chocolate from Belgium, and on and on and on.

New York is full of the most wonderful ethnic markets from which to garner specific ingredients. There are areas that have completely retained their ethnic nature. The Lower East Side of New York has sauerkraut still prepared the way it was a hundred or more years ago. Little Italy has wonderful fresh sausages and cheeses prepared on the premises by a son or daughter who has learned the recipe from a mother or grandmother. The tradition is upheld.

Cuisine, at best, can be only a language or a color palette, setting the groundwork from which cooks can begin to develop their own personal statements. I in no way intend to set firm ground rules with which to restrict people. To the contrary! This book is designed to bring the readers back in touch with basic principles. As an art, cooking requires visual and taste sensitivity . . . and it is chemistry, understanding how different elements affect one another not only from a taste standpoint or a color standpoint, but also from a textural standpoint.

It is important to learn the fundamentals of cooking, and to understand the impact of fine-quality ingredients.

In the next few chapters, it is my desire to introduce you to what may be a slightly different perspective. There are actions that many cooks are aware of, but they may not understand the reasons behind the action. They just do it because they have seen someone else do it, or because "that's the way they have always done it." Therefore they do not understand how to apply the same principles from dish to dish, nor do they understand when a step can be circumvented or when it is critical.

Once you learn to open your eyes to the cooking process, from selection to serving, and feel comfortable with your own interpretation of these steps, it becomes possible for a recipe to evolve.

Chapter I

Rack of Lamb with Rosemary and Garlic

Sensitivity

...understanding the elements

Philosopher-statesman Chuang Tsu said, "Ruling a large nation is like cooking a small fish. One must do it very gently." The purpose of this chapter is to reawaken, or possibly awaken for the first time, your sensitivity to some of the elements of cooking that have almost been lost in our modern time.

In order for a host or hostess to create a memorable evening, he or she must be in tune with the elements necessary to produce "magic." Whatever kind of occasion you are planning, whether business evening, or an evening "intime" . . . the ultimate goal is to bring joy. In order to accomplish this, the menu and all of the other elements must be considered. If the host or hostess spends the entire evening in the kitchen, the guests become aware of all the work and preparation that are going into the evening, and they become uncomfortable. However, when very close friends come for an evening or when it is just an evening at home, a complicated preparation in which everyone can be involved can itself create a beautiful and warm feeling.

Every element should be designed to enhance, not compete, with every other element. Like a conductor, the host or hostess should develop a program for an evening, encompassing how he or she would ideally like the evening to run and, then, conduct it from moment to moment. The show will run best when there is a flow and when it is simple, which is far more elegant than an unnecessarily complicated meal.

When planning a party for many guests, it is pure folly to attempt a complex dish, or one in which difficult or critical timing is necessary. For instance, if there is an abundance of time available, braising is a possibility. If there is only a short amount of preparation time available, sautéeing may be more appropriate. To ensure both that the evening progress comfortably and that the food be perfectly prepared, one cannot overlook any part of the planning or preparation. Each aspect is part of a total. The flowers and wine are every bit as important as individual dishes. Again, it is like conducting an orchestra: each aspect of the preparation of a meal must come together at the same moment, even though each element may have its own very different timing. Fish is one of the major challenges. Because fish has absolutely no tolerance for overcooking, it poses great difficulty—but, in the most positive way. Very frequently, a cook forgets that the cooking process continues after the fish (or meat) has been removed from the heat. Even placing it on a hot plate (which is absolutely necessary), continues the cooking process. The Orientals are masterful at this. They understand that the fish continues to cook all the way to the table.

Sensitivity to the evening as a whole must be taken into consideration. Obviously, certain assumptions must be made. A formal dinner party is best planned with an hour or an hour and a half for aperitif to ensure that guests are relaxed, yet not too sotted. A small or informal evening may have a longer aperitif hour, in which people are sipping their drinks and talking while watching the host prepare the food. One way or the other, the preparation and timing must have the flexibility to accommodate the unexpected.

Sensitivity also encompasses not calling attention to some change in the menu that must be made to accommodate a particular guest. For instance, if one of your guests is a vegetarian, the menu should be planned in such a way that no one is conscious of one guest having a particular dietary restriction, be it medical or self-imposed. The last thing you want is a discussion of why your guest is a vegetarian or of how long he has had "that problem!"

Fifth Avenue Oysters

This appetizer, while thoroughly delicious, is also the way to set the tone for an elegant dinner without complex or time-consuming preparation.

- 2 cloves garlic, very finely chopped
- 1 shallot, chopped medium fine
- 3 tablespoons unsalted butter
- 1/2 cup dry white wine
- 12 oysters
- 1/4 teaspoon black pepper, freshly ground
- 1/4 teaspoon dried oregano
- 2 fresh tomatoes, peeled, seeded, and chopped, or 2 Italian-style canned tomatoes, chopped
- 1/2 cup Gruyère cheese, coarsely grated
- 1/4 cup fine dry bread crumbs

Method

In a heavy-bottomed stainless steel skillet, melt the garlic and shallot in 2 tablespoons butter for about 8–10 minutes. Add the wine and bring up the heat. Reduce the liquid by half. Remove from heat.

Open the oysters, reserving the liquid. Strain the liquid and add it to the skillet. Add pepper, oregano, and chopped tomatoes. Cook for 5 minutes.

Place the oysters in the sauce.

Take a scant 1/2 cup Gruyère and sprinkle it over the mixture. Then sprinkle with bread crumbs, and dot with 1 tablespoon butter.

Place the skillet in a very hot oven for approximately 6 minutes. The highest heat is at the top of the oven, and therefore, the top rack is preferable for baking this dish. Then place under broiler for 2 minutes. The mixture should reduce further, be bubbling vigorously, and slightly crusted on the top. Serve on warm plates.

This is the kind of dish, like escargot, that has a sauce that is exquisite for dunking bread.

Yield: Two servings

Asparagus Maltaise

The addition of blood orange to the hollandaise in this recipe adds an unexpected taste, as well as a burst of color.

This recipe should be made with Spanish blood oranges whenever they are available, because of their wonderful taste and color.

- 1/2 cup orange juice, freshly squeezed
- 1/2 teaspoon orange rind, finely grated
- 1/2 cup hollandaise sauce (see page 207)
- 1 1/2 pounds fresh green or white asparagus, trimmed and peeled

Method

Prepare the hollandaise sauce.

In a noncorrosive pan, reduce the orange juice over medium heat to approximately 1/4 cup. Cool.

Fold the orange reduction and the rind into the hollandaise sauce.

Lightly steam the asparagus, or lightly cook them in boiling water, until they are *just* done. Arrange on a plate and spoon the sauce over.

Yield: Four servings

Artichoke Ragoût

2 artichokes
Juice of 1 lemon mixed with 1 cup water (acidulated water)
2 carrots, peeled
4 tiny new potatoes
1/4 cup lime juice
2 large pinches kosher salt
1 cup very light olive oil or soy oil
1 cup water
6 romaine lettuce leaves, washed

Method

Remove all the leaves from the artichokes, and cut the top tips, 1/4 inch down. Cut off all but 1/2 inch of the stem end. Peel off the dark green outer layer of skin, and with a spoon dig and remove the choke leaving only the heart. Dip the hearts in acidulated water.

Cut the carrots into 1 inch pieces on the diagonal.

Cut the potatoes in half.

Place the lime juice, salt, oil, and water in a small stainless steel skillet. Bring to a boil, and simmer until reduced to about 1 cup. It should begin to look opaque from the boiling process. Put the potatoes in the liquid, the carrots on top, and the artichokes in the center, leaning against each other. Cover with romaine leaves. Cover the skillet and simmer for 12–15 minutes.

To serve, lay the romaine leaves on a plate and arrange the vegetables on top. Spoon juices over.

Yield: Two servings

Note: This ragoût is delicious served hot, warm, or cold.

Chicken with Butter and Tarragon under the Skin Accompanied by Baby Carrots and Leeks

The technique used to insert the butter and tarragon under the skin of the chicken can be applied in a myriad of ways to vary the presentation and taste of many types of fowl. For instance, a truly elegant change is the substitution of foie gras and minced truffles under the skin of capon.

>
> Two 2 1/2-pound frying chickens, whole
> 1/2 cup unsalted cold butter, plus 4 tablespoons cut into 4 pieces
> 1/4 cup fresh tarragon leaves
> 1 cup chicken stock (see page 204)
> Kosher salt
> 1/2 teaspoon black pepper, freshly ground

Method

Prepare the chicken for roasting by folding the wings under and removing excess fat from both sides of the cavity. With the cavity facing you, push your fingers between the skin and the flesh of the breast. Gently ease the skin off the breast, creating a pocket. Push equal amounts of tarragon leaves under the skin of both birds.

Tie the birds around the thighs so that they will hold their shape while cooking. Smear each bird with 1 tablespoon butter. Place on a rack in a roasting pan and bake at 400° F. for about 35–40 minutes. After the first 15 minutes, baste with juices from the pan, and sprinkle each bird with a pinch of salt. After 40 minutes, check for doneness by moving a leg up and down. If it is done, it will move easily. You can also check by inserting a skewer into the thickest part of the thigh. If it is done, the juices will run yellow. If the bird is not cooked, the juices will run pink.

Remove from the oven, and pour the pan juices into a saucepan. Bring to a simmer, and skim off any fat that rises to the surface. Add the chicken stock. Simmer for an additional 10 minutes. Add salt, if necessary. Remove from heat.

Swirl in the remaining 2 tablespoons of butter and add the pepper. While the sauce is simmering and reducing, carve the chicken or split it in half.

Place the chicken on warm plates. Pour the hot juices over the chicken, and dress the plates with leeks and carrots.

Ingredients for the Leeks
- 4 leeks, white part only, well washed and split, but not separated
- 1/2 cup chicken stock (see page 204)
- Unsalted butter
- 1/2 teaspoon kosher salt

Method

Lay the leeks in a baking pan. Add the chicken stock and dot liberally with butter. Add salt, place on burner and bring to a simmer. Cover the pan tightly with a cover or aluminum foil.

Place in a 375° F. oven for 35–40 minutes. Check after 20 minutes. If the liquid has evaporated, add a little more stock. After 40 minutes check to see if a knife can easily pierce the ends of the leeks. The liquid should have reduced to a glaze. Remove from the oven.

Turn the leeks around in the liquid to coat and set them aside, partially covered, until needed.

Ingredients for the Carrots
- 20 tiny whole Belgian carrots, peeled
- 3/4 cup water
- 1 large pinch kosher salt
- 2 tablespoons unsalted butter

Method

Place the carrots in a small skillet with the water, salt, and butter. Bring to a medium simmer, and reduce heat slightly. Allow to simmer for 8–10 minutes. The liquid should almost entirely reduce, making a light glaze.

Remove from the heat. Turn the carrots in the glaze and set aside, partially covered, until needed.

Three to four minutes before you serve, place the leeks and carrots in their pans over gentle heat and heat until hot through.
Yield: Four servings

Variation

- Use fresh rosemary leaves in place of tarragon

Spinach Soup

This soup has an equally valid place on a formal or informal menu. The taste is rich, but it does not overwhelm.

    1   medium onion, sliced
    1 1/2   tablespoons unsalted butter
    2   pounds spinach, well washed, coarse stems removed and roughly chopped
    4   cups chicken stock (see page 204)
    2   cups water
    1   tablespoon kosher salt
    1   medium potato, peeled and roughly chopped
    1   pinch nutmeg
    6   tablespoons heavy cream or crème fraîche

Method

Melt onions in butter until they are translucent. Stir in the spinach, tossing it well in the butter. Cook for 2–3 minutes, until spinach wilts.

Add stock, water, salt, and potato. Bring to a gentle simmer for 15–20 minutes, or until the potato is soft.

Remove from the heat and allow to cool.

Purée the mixture in a food processor or blender.
Add nutmeg and taste for seasoning.
Ladle the soup into hot bowls. Spoon 1 1/2 tablespoons of cream or crème fraîche into the center of each bowl. Do not stir. Pass the peppermill.

Yield: Four servings

Terrine of Veal

The taste combination in this terrine is distinctive and intriguing. Because it must be prepared ahead it will help increase the time you have to spend with your guests.

2	pounds veal scallops, pounded quite thin
2	pounds bacon, thinly sliced
1	medium onion, finely chopped
1/4	cup parsley leaves, chopped
Freshly ground black pepper	
1/4	teaspoon rosemary
1/4	teaspoon thyme
1/4	teaspoon oregano
1/4	teaspoon basil
1/4	cup dried white wine

Method
Line a loaf pan with some of the bacon slices, allowing the ends of the bacon to hang over the sides of the pan.
Layer the veal scallops lengthwise, with alternating layers of bacon, onion, parsley, pepper, and crumbled herbs. Repeat until the terrine is full.
Lay the flaps of the lining bacon over the tops of the terrine.

Cover the top with additional bacon. Sprinkle white wine over the top. Bake in a 325° F. oven for 2 hours. Remove from the oven and place on a cookie sheet. Place a weight over the loaf and allow it to cool.

Refrigerate in the pan until quite cold. It must be served cold so the layers will hold together when sliced.

Yield: Four servings

Lobster Bisque

Truly one of the most sensuous soups in the world. The taste is both subtle and incredibly rich.

One 3-pound live lobster
3 tablespoons fine olive oil
1/3 cup leek, white part only, finely diced
1/2 cup onion, finely chopped
1/3 cup carrot, finely diced
2 1/2 cups dry white wine
3–4 sprigs fresh thyme or 1/4 teaspoon dried thyme
1 teaspoon garlic purée or 1 clove garlic, finely chopped
1 1/2 cups fish fumet (see page 202)
1 teaspoon kosher salt
1/4 teaspoon black pepper, freshly ground
1 bay leaf
2 ripe tomatoes, seeded, peeled, and chopped
3/4 cup heavy cream
3/4 cup half-and-half
1 teaspoon cognac
Reconstituted Japanese seaweed (Hijiki)

Method

Kill the lobster by placing a knife in the thorax and splitting it lengthwise. Remove the sack (queen) at the top of the head. Reserve the liver and the coral (dark green mass of eggs), if it has any, and place them in 2 tablespoons of white wine.

Separate the tail and legs from the body. Chop the thorax. Break the legs and tail into small pieces, but leave the claws whole. Save the juices with the liver and the coral.

Sauté the lobster with olive oil in a stainless steel skillet. Cook with high heat approximately 2 minutes, or until the lobster turns scarlet.

Add the leek, onion, and carrot. Cook, tossing and stirring until lightly browned, approximately 3 or 4 minutes. Make sure to stay with the pan, as it is at high heat.

Add the wine. Lower heat to gently simmer.

Add the thyme and stir in garlic purée. Add fish fumet, salt, pepper, and bay leaf. Simmer about 10 minutes.

Remove the lobster, except for the legs. Continue to simmer the sauce. Remove the lobster meat from the shells and return the shells, plus the chopped thorax, to the skillet while it continues to simmer. Stir in the tomatoes. Simmer for approximately 10 minutes. Strain through a fine sieve. Return to the heat and reduce to approximately 2 cups of liquid.

Purée the reserved liver (and coral) with the wine and stir into the liquid.

Add cream and half-and-half, and stir. Simmer gently for about 4–5 minutes.

Chop the lobster meat. Place a spoonful of lobster meat and 1/4 teaspoon cognac into each bowl. Ladle the hot soup over it. (This method prevents overcooking the lobster.) Place 4–5 strands of seaweed on top for color and texture.

Yield: Four servings

Rack of Lamb with Rosemary and Garlic

Rack of lamb is relatively simple to prepare, and always lends itself to elegant presentation.

> 1 tablespoon olive oil
> Kosher salt
> 1/4 cup red wine
> 1 1/2 teaspoons garlic purée (see page 217) or 1 teaspoon finely chopped fresh garlic
> 2-inch piece fresh rosemary, lightly bruised
> 1/4 cup glace de viande (see page 204) or 1 cup beef-veal stock (see page 203)
> 1 1/2 tablespoons unsalted butter
> Black pepper, freshly ground

Method

A full rack has 8 chops, but because they are very narrow, plan on one rack for two people. Have your butcher remove the chine bone, so that it will be easy to carve, trimming and preparing the lamb for the oven.

Preheat oven to 425° F. Cover the bones of the rack with a piece of aluminum foil. Brush the meaty side of the rack with olive oil and sprinkle lightly with salt. Place lamb on its flat side bones up on a rack in a roasting pan. Roast for 10–12 minutes. Then turn the lamb to lay meat side down and roast for another 10–12 minutes. This should produce medium rare lamb.

To check for doneness, the rack should be well browned on all sides, and the fattest part of the meat, in the center of the rack, should have a resistance and spring to it, but it should not be completely firm.

Remove the lamb from the oven. Take it out of the pan, and allow it to rest while you prepare the sauce.

Pour off any fat and deglaze the pan with the wine, scraping up all of the coagulated juices in the bottom of the pan. Pour through a fine sieve into a small saucepan. Stir in the garlic purée and bruised rosemary. Place over medium heat and cook for 2 minutes. Add the glace de viande or beef-veal stock and a pinch of salt. Let it simmer for 3–4 minutes. Pour any juices that have exuded from the lamb into the sauce. Simmer for another minute. (If you use the beef-veal stock, continue simmering until it is reduced to about 1/2 cup of liquid.) Remove the sprig of rosemary and set the sauce aside.

With a sharp knife, carve the rack into chops. You will see that the four center chops of each rack have an almost perfect appearance. Therefore I suggest putting two of the center chops forward on each plate, and placing two of the end chops behind. Return the sauce to a high heat, add pepper to taste, and quickly monter au beurre. Check for salt and spoon the sauce over the chops.

Yield: Four servings

Ragoût of Lobster on a Mound of Lingue di Passero

This dish takes relatively little actual preparation time; however, it requires the complete attention of the cook during certain steps. When including it on a dinner party menu balance it out with dishes that can be prepared in advance, such as a cold appetizer or soups.

Two 1 1/2-pound lobsters
2 tablespoons light olive oil
1 1/2 teaspoons shallot, finely chopped
1 1/2 teaspoons garlic purée
2 fresh tomatoes, peeled, seeded, and chopped, or 3 Italian-style canned tomatoes
1/4 cup cognac
1/4 cup dry white wine
1 large pinch kosher salt
4–5 fresh basil leaves, torn
3 grinds black pepper
4 tablespoons ice cold, unsalted butter, cut into chunks
1 pound lingue di passero or another fine-strand pasta, cooked al dente

Method

Plunge lobsters into boiling water for exactly 5 minutes. Cool under cold running water. Remove the meat from the shells and reserve the coral (the dark green mass of eggs), if it has any.

Place oil in a heavy-bottomed stainless steel skillet, and heat until quite hot. Add the lobster meat. Stir and cook for 1 minute. Add shallots and garlic, and if necessary, push the lobster away slightly to make sure that the shallots and garlic have contact with the bottom of the pan.

After cooking for 1 minute, stir and toss well. Remove the pan from the heat, and, averting your face, pour in the cognac. Return the pan to the heat, and cover it to put out the flame. Remove the cover, add wine, and simmer for about 1 minute. Add the tomatoes, salt, basil leaves, and pepper. Swirl the butter in very quickly. As soon as the butter has melted, pour over mounds of lingue di passero.

Yield: Four servings

Chapter II

Sparrows' Tongues (Linguine) with Avocado and Salsa

Selection

...the market speaks

One of the keys to understanding *New York Cuisine* and to being able to devise a menu that works is to permit the market and food products to speak for themselves.

With this sensitivity, you will find that each ingredient suggests itself. The first asparagus of the season, or a particularly beautiful yellow Dutch pepper, may serve as the jumping-off point for an entire dinner. The recipes in this section are designed to show how one element leads to another.

In New York I am fortunate to be able to shop at extraordinary stores like Balducci's, Zabar's, and Dean & Deluca, where an abundance of fresh produce and other products from all over the world are available throughout the year. I can buy wonderful strawberries twelve months of the year, snow peas, baby artichokes, different kinds of avocados, and African haricots verts, not just string beans! From day to day, there will be eight or nine different kinds of lettuce from which I can assemble different salads, each with a different balance of texture, color, and taste. I can add wonderful sour grasses and other greens that appear on the market. Smoked salmon, twelve kinds of pepperoni, Westphalian hams, fresh fish, aged meat, cheeses from all over the world, eight or nine types of dried mushrooms, fresh truffles—virtually everything one would ever want—are available from stores like Balducci's. More and more, many of these items are becoming available in major urban and suburban areas of the United States. This has provided options for the home cook that are tremendously exciting and allow for greater creativity.

It is a wonderful feeling to be able to walk into a market and look for colors and textures that suggest themselves. But if you need to shop in two or three stores, not knowing what one has and what the other doesn't, approach your menu by establishing the "givens." For instance, you pretty much know what the butcher will and will not have or what the fishmonger will or will not have. From this, you can decide what the main element will be. You should also remember that from a structural standpoint, all courses lead up to the main course and diminish from it. Once this concept is established, one can "filigree" around the main course with foods that suggest themselves to you in the market place. For instance, you may decide upon loin lamb chops. Then you go to the market and add succulent asparagus and oak mushrooms—possibly some truffles that have just arrived from Italy make you decide to prepare risotto as a side dish. Also, let things suggest themselves based upon what is already available in your larder. Many an exquisite dinner has been put together from food already on hand.

Virginia oak mushrooms have become available in the market. They are beautiful, and their taste is absolutely exquisite. Because of their musky flavor, a filet mignon with a red wine sauce might suggest itself. The oak mushrooms and filet mignon become the central focus, which can then be balanced with a pasta tossed with cream, butter, cracked black pepper, and freshly grated grana. On the other hand, a venison with szechuan, black, and green peppercorns needs a counterpoint to the richness of the venison—such as whole poached onions stuffed with vegetables and aromatics, and a compote of fresh sour cherries.

Wild Mushroom Soup

Each of the mushrooms in this soup is chosen for its taste, texture, and look.... The result is far more interesting than the familiar white domestic mushroom soup.

- 1 1/2 ounces dry morels
- 1 1/2 ounces dry porcini
- 1 cup white domestic mushrooms, thinly sliced
- 1 cup onion, thinly sliced
- 2 tablespoons unsalted butter
- 1 tablespoon clear oil, soy or corn
- 2 cups water
- 3 tablespoons glace de viande (see page 204) or 1/2 cup good beef stock (see page 203)
- 2 cups chicken stock (see page 204)
- 3 sprigs fresh thyme or 1/4 tablespoon dried thyme
- 1 bay leaf
- Kosher salt and pepper to taste
- 1 tablespoon flat parsley, roughly chopped

Method

Rinse well and trim the morels and porcini. Reconstitute them by soaking each in 3/4 cup of warm water.

Melt the onions in butter and oil. Sauté the white mushrooms with the onions for about 2–3 minutes. Add the chicken stock, water, and glace de viande or beef stock.

Strain 1 cup of the water from the reconstituted morels and porcini. Add this and the reconstituted mushrooms to the white mushrooms and onions, along with the thyme and bay leaf. Simmer for about 20 minutes. Correct seasoning.

At this point, the soup is a clear broth with beautiful layers of mushrooms floating throughout. Sprinkle with fresh parsley.

Yield: Four servings

Variation

- Take half of the solid ingredients and purée them in a food processor. Then stir them back into the soup.
- Add 1/2 cup heavy cream and heat through.

Poached Pears

Beautiful fresh pears and succulent raspberries combine in this dessert to create a taste that is more than the sum of the parts.

    4   pears, firm, ripe, and unblemished (preferably with a stem)
    Juice of 1 lemon in 1 cup water (acidulated water)
    3/4 bottle full-bodied red wine
    3   tablespoons sugar
    Juice of 1 lemon
    1   cinnamon stick
    1/4 pint fresh raspberries
    3   ounces Framboise de Bourgogne or Cassis
    1   cup heavy cream, lightly whipped

Method

    With a vegetable peeler, carefully remove all the skin from each pear so that there is a clean, even surface. Do not remove the stem. Dip in acidulated water (see page 221) to prevent pears from browning. They should remain in the water until you are ready to poach them.

    Take a fork with sharp tines and gently score each pear from top to bottom, following the natural contour. In a saucepan make a solution with red wine, sugar, lemon juice, and a cinnamon stick.

Add the pears and poach them over moderate heat for approximately 15–20 minutes or until just soft. Take care that they do not become mushy.

Remove the pan from the heat, and let the pears cool in the liquid for approximately 20 minutes. This sets the color. Then remove the pears from the liquid with a slotted spoon, and drain them on a rack with a dish underneath to catch the excess liquid.

Strain the wine mixture and return it to a moderate heat. Reduce the liquid to a syrup. Remove from the heat and let it cool.

After it has cooked, drizzle the syrup over the pears while they are still draining on the rack. This will glaze the pears.

Soak the raspberries in the framboise for one or two hours. Pour the mixture into a food processor and purée. Strain through a fine sieve to remove the seeds.

Make a pool of raspberry purée in each dish. Put a dollop of lightly whipped cream in the center. Place a pear in the middle of the pool of cream. Drizzle some of the cream half-way down the side of the pear, and allow it to run into the pool of cream.

Yield: Four servings

Sparrows' Tongues (Linguine) with Avocado and Salsa

While the "hot" of jalapeño peppers is the main thrust of this eclectic pasta, there are taste and texture balances in the avocado, corn, cheese, tomatoes, and tortilla chips. Each ingredient is important on many levels, not the least of which is balance.

1 ripe avocado
Juice of 1 lemon
1 green chili pepper (see below)
3 fresh green jalapeño peppers
2 light yellow jalapeño peppers (if not available, use 2 additional green jalapeño peppers)
2 hot red peppers
1/2 cup water
1 tablespoon white vinegar
1/2 teaspoon kosher salt
3 tablespoons light olive oil
1 onion, medium chopped
2 tablespoons garlic purée
3 fresh tomatoes or 4 canned Italian-style tomatoes, peeled, seeded, and chopped
5 ounces Sacramento tomato juice
3 ears fresh corn, niblets removed
1/2 teaspoon cumin seed
2 tablespoons fresh parsley, finely chopped
1 pound linguine
3/4 cup good Fontina cheese, coarsely grated
1 handful tortilla chips
8 scallions, well washed and trimmed

If fresh peppers are not available, use the ones that come in jarred varieties, but be sure to maintain the color balance of the dish.

If fresh corn is not available, good-quality frozen corn can be used. Of course, the quality of the taste and the texture will be somewhat changed.

Method

Cut the avocado in half lengthwise. Then take a knife and with a light blow crosswise, embed the blade of the knife into the pit of the avocado. Turn it slightly and the stone of the avocado will come out cleanly. To remove the skin of the avocado, score the length of the skin, and beginning at the pointed end of the avocado, peel off the skin as you would a banana. (This will work only with well-ripened avocados.) Cut the avocado into cubes. Sprinkle well with lemon juice and set aside.

Finely mince all the peppers. Blend the water, vinegar, and salt, and add the peppers. Allow the mixture to marinate for 30 minutes.

Pour olive oil into a large skillet on a medium heat. Add the chopped onions and garlic. Cook gently until they are translucent, approximately 8–10 minutes. Then add the tomatoes and cook for about 2–3 minutes. The mixture at this point should start to bubble moderately. The tomatoes will soften and release their juices. Add the tomato juice to the pan. Let it continue to simmer for 8–10 minutes over medium heat.

Stir the corn niblets into the tomato mixture, and cook for 1 minute.

Add the cumin. Cook on a low heat, and stir in the parsley and avocados. Cook for two minutes. Remove from the heat and set aside. Strain the pepper mixture and pour the liquid into the sauce. Stir quickly. The sauce should be the consistency of tomato purée, neither too thick nor too thin.

To a large pan of boiling salted water, add the pasta. Make sure to stir the pasta once it is in the boiling water so that it does not stick. Cook until the pasta is al dente, or for approximately 5–6 minutes. Drain well.

Place small mounds of pasta on warmed plates. Spoon sauce over and sprinkle with grated cheese. Crush the tortilla chips in your hand, and sprinkle them over each dish. Encircle the pasta with scallions, and serve.

Cold beer is the best beverage to accompany this dish.

Yield: Four servings

Virginia Oak Mushrooms with Shallots

Virginia oak mushrooms have only recently become available on almost a year-around basis. Their muskiness gives them an extraordinary character which is well able to stand on its own with just the addition of some shallots, butter, and oil.

- 2 tablespoons fine olive oil
- 1 tablespoon unsalted butter
- 8–12 whole mushrooms, cleaned
- 1 tablespoon shallot, finely chopped
- 3 sprigs fresh thyme or 1/4 teaspoon dried thyme
- Kosher salt
- Pepper to taste

Method

In a heavy-bottomed skillet, heat the oil and butter until they are almost smoking. Add the mushrooms, and toss to coat them with oil and butter. Move them around in the pan to prevent their sticking or burning, but allow them to sauté for about 3 minutes. Add the shallots and thyme. Stir well. Sauté for another 2 minutes. Remove from the heat. Season with salt and pepper. Serve on very warm plates.

Yield: Four servings

Filets of Striped Bass with Sweet Peppers, Lime, and Cream

The combination with sweet pepper, an unexpected bit of lime, and cream produces a sophisticated blend of tastes and colors.

> 4 filets of striped bass, 6 or 7 ounces each
> 1/2 cup dry white wine
> 1/4 cup water
> 1/2 cup fish fumet (see page 202)
> 1 teaspoon shallot, finely chopped
> 1/2 cup sweet red pepper, medium diced
> 2 teaspoons lime juice
> 1/4 teaspoon lime rind, grated
> 3/4 cup heavy cream
> 1/2 teaspoon kosher salt
> 4 to 5 grinds black pepper, freshly cracked
> 1 1/2 tablespoons unsalted butter

Method

Make sure that all fish bones are removed (a tweezer is helpful). Poach the striped bass in white wine, water, fumet, and shallots (see page 214). Remove to a platter and cover loosely.

Rapidly reduce the poaching liquid to about 1/2 cup. Add the sweet pepper, lime juice, rind, and cream. Stir. Add salt and pepper, and cook over medium heat until slightly thickened. It should be slightly syrupy, but not thick. Pour the liquid that has drained from the fish into the sauce, and cook a minute or two more.

Check for seasoning, then swirl the butter into the hot sauce. Place filets on heated plates, and spoon the sauce over.

Yield: Four servings

Double-Baked Potato and Leek Soufflé

Leeks and potatoes are delicious in almost any form. Here they are assembled with some cream and fine grana in a soufflé.

Soufflés intimidate some of the best chefs because of their tendency to collapse at the slightest wrong move, not to mention falling shortly after being removed from the oven. This recipe removes all fears from the preparation of a soufflé. Because of the double baking process and the addition of cream, the soufflé comes to the table puffy and delicious.

This soufflé, and its variations, is particularly delicious served with roasted meats. It can also be served for lunch or brunch, accompanied by a green salad or lightly blanched vegetables.

- 1/2 cup potatoes, in 1/2-inch cubes
- 1 leek, white part only, well washed, thinly sliced
- 2 tablespoons unsalted butter
- 3 tablespoons flour
- 3/4 cup milk
- 3 eggs, separated
- 1 pinch kosher salt
- 6 grinds black pepper
- 3/4 cup heavy cream
- 1/2 cup grana, finely grated

Method

Simmer the potatoes in well-salted water to cover, until they are cooked through but still firm. Remove from the heat, rinse under cold water, and dry.

Simmer the leeks in lightly salted water for 10 minutes, drain well, and set aside.

Melt the butter over gentle heat, and whisk in the flour. Cook slowly for 2–3 minutes, making sure it does not discolor. Remove from heat. Heat the milk to a simmer, and add it all at once to the flour mixture. Whisk vigorously. Return the mixture to the heat, and cook for 2–3 minutes, stirring constantly, until it thickens considerably. Remove from the heat and add the egg yolks, one at a time, whisking well after each addition.

Fold in the potatoes, leeks, and pepper.

Beat the egg whites with a pinch of salt until they are stiff but not dry. *Stir* one-quarter of the beaten egg white mixture into the potato mixture. After this is combined, *gently fold* the remaining egg whites into the potatoes.

Pour the mixture into a well-buttered 1-quart mold, or divide it among six individual buttered molds. Gently smooth the surface, and place the mold or molds in a bain-marie. A bain-marie can be made by putting the mold or molds into another pan large enough to enable you to pour hot water 3/4 up the height of the mold. Place the bain-marie with the molds in a 350° F. oven. Bake for 20–25 minutes. Check occasionally to make sure the water does not boil. When done, the soufflé should be puffed, lightly browned, and in the center gently firm to the touch.

Carefully remove the bain-marie from the oven. Then remove the molds from the bain-marie. Allow them to rest for 15 minutes, or if they do not have to be used immediately, allow them to cool completely.

Run a thin-bladed knife around the edge of the soufflé, then unmold onto an ovenproof plate or pan. Spoon the cream over the top, and sprinkle on the grated grana. Bake in a 450° F. oven for about 15 minutes, or until it repuffs and becomes a beautiful golden brown. Remove from the oven. With a wide spatula, place on a heated plate, and serve.

To make this dish more elegant, you can turn the soufflé, after the second baking, into a fully baked savory tart shell (see page 212). There are many variations for this dish.

Yield: Four servings

Variations

- Add 1/4 to 1/2 cup smoked salmon, chopped.
- Add 1/2 cup sliced oak mushrooms, sautéed in 2 tablespoons butter with 1 shallot, finely chopped

- Add 1/2 cup sweet red peppers, skinned, seeded, and chopped, or any other sweet pepper, lightly cooked in 2 tablespoons butter with 1 shallot, finely chopped
- Add 1/2 cup blanched asparagus tips.
- Spoon 1 teaspoon fine caviar over each individual soufflé, after it is baked the second time.
- Add 1/2 cup double-smoked bacon, diced, sautéed, and drained well, or 1/2 cup prosciutto, finely chopped. Top with a generous sprinkling of grated mozzarella, then grana, before the second baking.
- Add 1/2 cup shrimp, cleaned, deveined, and roughly chopped.

Filets of Sole with Cucumber, Crème Fraîche, and Fresh Mint

There are some ingredients that are always refreshing; certainly cucumbers and fresh mint fall within that category. This filet of sole has a unique bright, fresh taste.

    1 medium cucumber, peeled, split in half lengthwise and seeded
Four filets of sole, 6 to 7 ounces each
1/2 cup water
1/2 cup dry white wine
1 tablespoon shallot, chopped
3/4 cup crème fraîche (see page 218)
5 medium-size fresh mint leaves, torn, plus 8 perfect whole leaves
1 teaspoon kosher salt
1/4 teaspoon white pepper, ground
2 tablespoons unsalted butter

Method

Split cucumbers in half lengthwise again, and then cut each piece into 3 long strips. Then cut across into 2-inch pieces.

Fold filets in half horizontally, skinned side in. Place in a stainless steel skillet and add water and white wine. Sprinkle with shallots, and heat to below a simmer. Gently poach (see page 214) for about 5 minutes, never allowing the liquid to boil.

Remove the filets to a warm plate and cover loosely.

Add the cucumbers to the skillet, turn the heat up, and reduce the liquid to about 5 tablespoons. Add the crème fraîche, simmer and reduce until the sauce begins to thicken. Add torn mint leaves, salt, and white pepper. Stir well. Pour liquid released from the fish into the cream. Cook about 3 minutes. Remove from heat and swirl in the butter.

Place each filet in the center of a heated plate. Spoon sauce over the filets and arrange with 2 mint leaves per filet.

Yield: Four servings

Torta

In a sense, this is the original cheesecake!

Many gourmet shops have taken this idea from the Italians, and these delicious cheeses are becoming more widely available.

For the basic preparation, alternate layers of Mascarpone cheese with other ingredients (see below) in a layer-cake fashion. Then wrap it tightly and chill it, to help marry the flavors. The possibilities for assembling are endless, so let your imagination run wild! When you have wonderful fresh ingredients, the results will be magnificent.

- Torta Basil: Alternate layers of Mascarpone with thin layers of Gorgonzola, freshly torn basil leaves, and a sprinkling of pignoli nuts. The top layer should be Mascarpone.
- Torta Salmon: Alternate Mascarpone with layers of smoked salmon.
- Torta Rambolle: Alternate Mascarpone with layers of Rambolle cheese.
- Torta with Black Truffles: Sprinkle thinly sliced black truffles between layers of Mascarpone.
- Alternate layers of Mascarpone with pitted black or green olives.
- Alternate layers of Mascarpone with layers of salmon caviar.

If fresh Mascarpone is not available at your local cheese store, you can substitute a fine cream cheese; however, this will change the richness and lightness of the taste.

Mussel Soup

These tastes are classic in combination. The intention of this soup is seen in the selection of herbs and spices. The addition of the saffron alone produces a subtly exotic taste.

For the Mussels
- 1/4 cup water
- 2 pounds mussels, well scrubbed and rinsed
- 1/2 cup dry white wine
- 1 tablespoon shallot, finely chopped

For the Soup
- 1 tablespoon garlic purée or 2 cloves garlic, finely chopped
- 1/2 onion, chopped
- 1 leek, white part only, well cleaned and chopped
- 1/4 cup olive oil
- 2 fresh tomatoes, peeled, seeded, and chopped, or 3 canned Italian-style plum tomatoes
- 1 large pinch saffron
- 2-inch piece fresh orange rind
- 1 bay leaf
- 3 sprigs fresh thyme or 1/4 teaspoon dried thyme
- 3 cups fish fumet (see page 202)
- 1/4 teaspoon fennel seed, ground or chopped
- 3–4 parsley stems, leaves removed (reserve leaves)
- 8 black peppercorns
- 1/2 cup heavy cream
- Kosher salt to taste
- Garlic croûtons (see page 218)

Method

Place water, mussels, wine, and shallots in a pot. Cover and place over high heat. Steam the mussels open for about 4 minutes. Remove the pot from the heat. Take the mussels from the broth, remove them from the shell, and allow to cool.

Strain the cooking liquid through three thicknesses of cheesecloth or linen, making sure that all sediment is completely removed. Pour into a saucepan and put aside.

Sauté the garlic, onion, and leek in olive oil until melted or about 12 minutes. Add this to the mussel broth, along with the tomatoes, saffron, orange rind, bay leaf, thyme, fish fumet, fennel, parsley stems, and peppercorns. Bring to a simmer, and cook for about 30 minutes.

Strain the broth and boil it rapidly for 5 minutes.

Add the cream and simmer for 2 minutes. (Before you add the cream, if the broth does not have the intensity of taste desired, allow it to reduce a while longer. Then add the cream.) Taste for salt.

Ladle into hot bowls; add 4 or 5 shelled mussels and a fresh garlic croûton to each. Sprinkle with parsley leaves.

Yield: Four servings

Lobster, Shrimp, Scallops, and Leeks

When you combine good ingredients the results will be good . . . and lobster, shrimp, and scallops combined in almost any variation produce extraordinary results. The addition of fresh basil, tomatoes, and cognac accentuates the innate sweetness of these particular shellfish, and creates a flavor that moves far beyond extraordinary to fine.

> One 2-pound lobster
> 8 medium-size shrimp (16's)
> 2 tablespoons olive oil
> 1/2 pound sea scallops, cut into thirds
> 2 teaspoons garlic purée or 1/2 teaspoon garlic, finely chopped
> 1 tablespoon shallot, finely chopped
> 1 leek, white part only, well cleaned and julienned
> 3 tablespoons good cognac
> 2 fresh tomatoes, peeled, seeded, and chopped, or 3 canned Italian-style plum tomatoes, chopped
> 1/4 cup dry white wine
> 8 tablespoons unsalted cold butter, cut into 4 pieces
> Kosher salt
> Coarsely ground black pepper
> 12 leaves fresh basil, or 1/2 teaspoon dried basil

Method

Plunge lobster into boiling salted water and cook for 5 minutes. Remove and cool under cold running water. Split the lobster down the center. Remove lobster meat from the claws, tail, and knuckles, as well as any meat that is remaining in the thorax. Cut meat into bite-size pieces.

Shell and devein the shrimp. Cut them in half lengthwise.

Before proceeding, make sure that all the other ingredients are prepared, as this is a very fast dish, and timing is of great importance.

In a heavy-bottomed stainless steel skillet, heat the olive oil until it is about to smoke. Toss in the lobster, shrimp, scallops, garlic, shallot, and leek. Stir quickly to coat the ingredients with the oil and to prevent their burning. Cook for a total of about 1 1/2 minutes. Remove from the heat, and with your face averted, add the cognac, flame, and douse the flame by covering it. Return to heat. Add the tomatoes and wine. Stir, and cook 3 minutes.

Swirl in the butter and stir for about 1 1/2 minutes.

Add salt and pepper to taste. Tear basil leaves into small pieces and then stir them into the mixture.

This dish can be served with lightly cooked vegetables, or over lightly seasoned ricotta-filled ravioli.

Yield: Four servings

Wild Rice with Apricots and Hazelnuts

The sweet nuttiness of the wild rice and hazelnuts is balanced by the tartness of the apricot.

> 1/2 pound wild rice (see page 215)
> 2 tablespoons unsalted butter
> 1/2 teaspoon kosher salt
> Ground black pepper to taste
> 3 dried apricots, chopped
> 2 tablespoons hazelnuts, chopped

Method
Rinse the rice in cold water, then place it in a small pot with a heavy lid. Add enough water to cover the rice, plus 3/4 inch.

Place on a high heat and bring to a boil. Immediately turn it down to a gentle simmer, cover tightly, and cook gently for about 35 minutes.

Check the rice to see if there is still liquid by gently pushing back the grains with a fork to see the bottom of the pan. Take care not to disturb the rice too much. If the liquid has evaporated and the rice is not cooked, add 1/4 cup water and cook until done.

When the rice is done, add the butter, salt, and pepper to taste, and stir. Then stir in the bits of apricots and hazelnuts.

Yield: Four servings

Seafood Lasagne

This approach to lasagne moves far away from the traditional tomato and meat versions. The ricotta, pasta, and velouté become exquisite platforms for shrimp, clams, and mussels.

Ingredients for Steaming the Clams and Mussels
- 1   dozen clams, medium sized, well washed
- 2   pounds mussels, scrubbed
- 1/4   cup white wine
- 1/4   cup water
- 1   shallot, chopped

Ingredients for the Lasagne
- 1   pound fresh lasagne noodles, or 1 pound dry, cooked in boiling salted water, al dente
- 1   pound ricotta cheese
- Black pepper, freshly ground
- 1/2   pound shrimp, peeled, deveined, and roughly chopped

Velouté (see page 206; use the liquids from steaming the mussels and clams as your liquid in the velouté)
2 sprigs fresh tarragon leaves or 1/4 teaspoon dried tarragon
1 cup peeled, chopped, and seeded tomatoes, or 5 Italian-style canned plum tomatoes, well drained and chopped
1/2 cup grana, grated
2 tablespoons unsalted butter
2 pounds spinach (see page 214)

Method

Combine the wine, water, and shallot in a saucepan and steam open the clams. Combine same amounts of ingredients and steam open the scallops. Remove them from the shells. Discard shells and reserve the cooking liquids. Strain the liquids for use in the velouté.

Line the bottom of a 9-inch square baking pan with overlapping layers of the noodles. (If fresh lasagne noodles are used, they need not be cooked.) Spread a thin layer of the ricotta cheese on top of the noodles. Grind black pepper over the cheese. Place one quarter of the velouté sauce over the seafood. Sprinkle with a few tarragon leaves. Repeat these layers; however, place the tomatoes in the center layer. End with a layer of noodles, which should just reach the top of the pan.

Sprinkle the grana on top and lightly dot with butter.

Cook in a 375° F. oven for 35–40 minutes, until the top is lightly browned and bubbling. Remove from the oven and let sit for 10–15 minutes, to allow the contents to settle.

Serve within a circle of lightly cooked spinach.

Yield: Four servings

Variations

- Lobster lightly cooked, removed from the shell and roughly chopped
- Oysters removed from the shell
- Back-fin lump crab

Chapter III

Seafood, Broccoli Rabe, Potato, and Rosemary Pizzas

Tonic Chord

...rediscovering the essence

George Balanchine used to say that he rarely choreographed to the music of Bach because "Vat could you do—it vould be like geelding the leely!" Over the years, many dishes have lost their true personality, because the wrong element has taken over, and the purpose of the entire dish has been misunderstood. Frequently—like choreographing to Bach—people do not know when something is complete in and of itself. This chapter is designed to help you explore a dish—to determine what can be edited away, what is essential, and what can be meaningfully added. This essence, the tonic chord, is the keystone to the total structure.

Bouillabaisse—La Bouillabaisse, La Vrai Bouillabaisse—has been discussed and argued over, probably for centuries. But as important as the choice of fish may be, a fine broth and a traditional rouille, including sea urchin, tie the dish together. The tonic chord is the broth and rouille. Once that is comprehended, the dish can evolve according to individual taste, and the availability of ingredients. However, it will not be a La Vrai Bouillabaisse unless certain fish, which are generally available only near Marseilles, are used.

Pasta is not usually thought of as having a significant flavor. But in reality, it is the tonic chord of any pasta dish. Since much of the commercially made American pasta is virtually tasteless, many Americans have never experienced what a fine pasta can be. However, more and more frequently, fine Italian brands, such as

De Cecco and Agnesi, are available in food stores and supermarkets. Good quality American pasta can be used, but take special care not to cook beyond *al dente*. Sauces should be chosen with the individual shape of the pasta in mind. Very thin pasta like *capellini* requires a sauce that is thin enough to drizzle down through the strands of pasta to wet it while trapping the tastes (mushrooms, shellfish, etc.) on top. Wider cuts, such as *penne*, are normally served with a sauce that clings to the surfaces of the pasta. Shells and *rigatoni* have areas that entrap sauce; they are normally tossed well with sauce, then additional sauce is spooned on top, and sprinkled with an herb. Since it is the pasta that is primary, it becomes vulgar to have it swimming in sauce. The sauces in this and other chapters have a richness which would make it overwhelming if too much sauce were added to the pasta.

Americans have over the years become convinced that fat, in and of itself, is bad, so they are afraid or intimidated in their use of fat. However, the difference between a good pâte and one that is flat is the liberal use of fat—again, the tonic chord.

For curry, understanding the progression of the different tastes is the tonic chord. This enables one to effectively "take the heat off one's mouth" and maximize the taste contrasts. The curry dish is most successful when complemented by certain other dishes, such as cucumber and yogurt salad, to cool the palate and prepare it for the next bite.

Seafood Ravioli

The tonic chord of this dish is the pasta. All of the ingredients will fall short of their intended result if the pasta is tasteless or overcooked.

Ingredients for Pasta (see page 215)

Ingredients for Ravioli Filling
- 1/4 pound fresh wild mushrooms such as oak, pleurote, or chanterelle
- 1 tablespoon light olive oil
- 1 tablespoon unsalted butter
- 1 shallot, finely chopped
- 1 leek, white part only, well washed and chopped
- One 1 1/2-pound lobster
- 5 ounces filet of sole
- 1 teaspoon kosher salt
- 1 small pinch cayenne pepper
- 1/2 cup heavy cream
- 1/4 pound bay scallops
- 1/4 pound shrimp, cleaned, deveined, and chopped
- Egg wash (see page 221)

Method

Sauté the mushrooms for approximately 2 minutes in oil and butter over high heat. Toss often. Add shallot and toss to make sure the pieces make contact with the pan. Cook another 2 minutes. Remove from heat and allow to cool.

Simmer the leek in a small amount of lightly salted water for about 8–10 minutes. Drain and cool.

Plunge lobster into rapidly boiling salted water and cook for 5 minutes. Run under cold water to cool. Split lengthwise and discard the queen. Remove the meat from the tail and claws.

Reserve the roe, if there is any, and the liver. Chop the lobster meat.

Purée the sole in a food processor with half the lobster meat, liver, salt, and cayenne. Slowly add cream.

Combine the purée with the scallops, shrimp, and remaining chopped lobster meat. Stir in the mushrooms and leek. Chill for 1 hour.

Divide the pasta in half. Roll out one half as thin as possible.

Form heaping-tablespoon-size balls of the seafood mixture and place them 2 inches apart on the dough. There should be room for 12 mounds of the mixture.

With a pastry brush, paint egg wash in a crosshatch pattern across the dough, and between all of the mounds. This will act as a sealing agent for the ravioli.

Roll out the other ball of dough and carefully place it over the mounds. Using the long handle of a wooden spoon, gently but firmly press down—and thereby seal—along the crosshatching. Be sure to press and seal well. You can also use your fingers.

With a knife or rolling cutter, cut the ravioli apart along the sealed lines. Gently press the edges of each ravioli to make sure that they are completely sealed.

Place them on a plate and cover with plastic wrap. Refrigerate for 20 minutes. If they are not going to be used immediately, sprinkle the ravioli generously with coarsely ground cornmeal to prevent sticking.

Drop the ravioli into a large pot of boiling salted water. After the water returns to a boil, continue to cook for 3–4 minutes. Remove the ravioli with a slotted spoon and drain well.

Place the ravioli on heated plates and spoon beurre blanc (see page 209) or a warm tomato sauce over (see page 210). Pass the peppermill.

If there was coral, or roe, in the lobster, purée it with 2 tablespoons butter. Swirl the lobster butter through the beurre blanc, and heat it gently until the coral turns pink.

Yield: Four servings

Pizza Crust

The secret to good pizza is the crust. This is a very simple recipe, but it will give you a crust that is excellent for a myriad of topping variations. It is important that the pizza be cooked either on a pizza stone or on quarry tiles that have been placed on the rack of your oven and heated well.

1 teaspoon yeast
3/4 cup warm water
3 cups unbleached flour
1 1/2 teaspoons kosher salt
1 tablespoon olive oil
Stone-ground cornmeal

Method
Sprinkle the yeast over the surface of warm water to dissolve. Let it sit for 5 minutes, until the yeast is activated.

Sift the flour and salt together. Stir the yeast mixture into the flour. Then add the olive oil and continue to stir until it forms a fairly loose mass, adding more water if necessary. Turn onto a well-floured board. Flour your hands, and then knead the dough about 10 to 15 times. Form the dough into a ball and cover it with either a towel or bowl. Let it sit for 1–1 1/2 hours, until it doubles in width. (Note: This dough will not rise in height very much.)

Liberally sprinkle a pizza paddle with coarsely-ground cornmeal to prevent dough from sticking.

Take one-quarter of the dough in your floured hands and pull, stretch, and pinch it. Close your eyes and think of the pizza men that you have seen so often. Form a thin 10-inch circle of dough with slightly thicker edges. The thinness is very important. Place the dough on the paddle and cover with a pushing, nudging motion, slip the pie onto the preheated pizza stone. Bake at 450° F. for between 12–15 minutes. Then slip the paddle under the pizza and remove it from the oven.

Pizza toppings

- Spread the dough with 1 tablespoon garlic purée to within 1 inch of the edge. Add 6 dollops, approximately 1 teaspoon each, of Beurre de Chèvre or chèvre cheese, spaced evenly over the pie. Sprinkle liberally with fresh rosemary and grind black pepper on top. Sprinkle with 1 tablespoon olive oil.
- Seafood Pizza: Thoroughly wash and scrub 6 mussels and 4 clams in their shells. Clean shrimp, but leave the tail shells on. Spread a thin layer of tomato sauce (see page 210) on the crust to within 1 inch of the edge. Arrange the mussels, clams, and shrimp, in their shells, on the sauce. Sprinkle with grana, salt, and pepper. Drizzle with olive oil. Bake 12–15 minutes, or until the shells open. Not only does this pie look beautiful, and most unusual, but it also becomes wonderful finger food. As each clam and mussel is removed, it leaves a "tidal pool" filled with the delicious juices mixing with the tomato sauce.
- Tomato sauce with lightly sautéed mushrooms, lightly sautéed pepperoni, or lightly sautéed sweet peppers.
- On top of any of the red pizzas previously mentioned, you can sprinkle mozzarella, smoked mozzarella, or grana.
- White Pizza: 1/16-inch thick slice raw potatoes, rinsed and dried. Arrange slices on top of pizza, slightly overlapping. Sprinkle with olive oil, salt, pepper, and fresh rosemary.
- 1/2 cup ricotta and 1/4 cup grana mixed and spread over the dough. Sprinkle with lightly steamed vegetables, such as broccoli or broccoli-rabe. Add garlic, salt, and pepper.
- Cover dough with thick slices of fresh tomato, placing a leaf of fresh basil under each slice. Sprinkle with oil, salt, pepper, and grana.

Raspberry Fruit Tarts with Chocolate

Pastry crusts, like pizza crusts, are the jumping-off point for a perfect tart or pie. If it is tasteless it serves no positive purpose other than to contain the filling. At its best it is light, flaky, and distinctive on its own, and needs little adornment.

      Pastry dough (see page 212), or puff pastry can be used
      1   pint fresh raspberries

Ingredients for Glaze
      2   ounces bittersweet chocolate
      1/2 cup clear red currant jelly or raspberry preserves, strained through a sieve, or 1 cup clear red currant jelly if chocolate is not used
      Optional: Fresh mint leaves

Method

    Roll out the dough to 1/16-inch thickness. Cut circles that are 1 inch larger than individual tart pans. Line each pan with the dough, but be careful not to stretch it. Make sure that it conforms to the sides of the pan. To avoid stretching or making holes, use a 2-tablespoon piece of dough dipped in flour to push the crust against the sides of the pans.

    Freeze the crusts until they are solid. Remove the pans from the freezer and pierce the dough with the tines of a fork. Bake at 425° F. for 10–12 minutes, until they are golden brown.

    Remove the tart shells, cool them on a rack, then remove them from the tart pans.

    Prefreezing should hold the crust and prevent it from collapsing during the cooking process. However, instead of this method, each shell can be lined with waxed paper and filled with beans or rice before baking. You can also place another tart pan of the same size inside the shell. Remove the second tart pan after baking for 5 minutes. Yet another method is to place the circles of dough over the bottoms of a muffin tin. Freeze, then remove and prick with the tines of a fork. Bake upside down in the oven.

Chop the chocolate into small pieces. Melt it in a double boiler, *over, not in,* gently simmering water. Never let the water boil! Another gentle method for melting chocolate is to place it in a bowl in the oven with only a pilot light on. It will melt in about 45 minutes.

Since the shells are very fragile, you must work carefully when painting their insides. Use a pastry brush to paint the chocolate over the bottom and the interior sides, up to 1/4 inch from the top of the shell. This will waterproof the crust and keep the pastry flaky. The other way of sealing the crust is to melt the jelly or preserves in a small saucepan over medium heat. Gently simmer for about 1 minute or until it thickens slightly and becomes sticky. Allow to cool for 1–2 minutes and apply with a pastry brush to seal the bottoms and sides.

Pick over the berries, and arrange them in the shells in a single layer, with the tops of the raspberries up. Completely cover the bottom of the shell with berries, and then arrange a second layer. Using a pastry brush, gently dribble the red glaze back and forth over the raspberries. Place a mint leaf on the top.

Variations

- Glaze with currant jelly to seal, then allow to cool. Add crème fraîche which has been beaten with heavy cream. Top with berries.
- Spoon a light custard on top of the glaze before adding berries.
- Dip whole peaches in boiling water for about a minute, then gently slip off the skins. Cut the peaches in half following their natural seam, and remove the pit. Make a ball of almond paste large enough to fit the cavity left by the peach pit. (Almond paste can be purchased at most supermarkets and fine food purveyors. For a substitute, mix 1/4 cup ground almonds with 1 teaspoon soft unsalted butter and 1 teaspoon Amaretto di Sarrono.) Spoon crème

fraîche that's been lightly mixed with heavy cream onto the bottom of the glazed shell. Place the peach, cavity side down, in the tart shell. For a glaze for the peach, use apricot preserves, pushed through a sieve. If the glaze becomes too thick, it can be heated to thin it slightly. Note: Red currant is generally used as the glaze for red fruits. Apricot preserves are normally used as the glaze for orange or yellow fruits.
- These tarts can be varied by cutting the dough or puff pastry into oblong or other artful shapes. Paint the sides of the dough with water in order to make them sticky. Make braids or other shapes to create a border to hold the fruit. Cook these shapes on a cookie sheet after freezing. Proceed with the recipe in the same manner as the tarts.

Snails in Garlic Cream

Snails are often prepared with garlic. This dish permits the garlic to project itself with a profound richness.

1/2 cup hollandaise sauce. Prepare first (Omit lemon juice listed in recipe. See page 207).
24 snails
1 tablespoon garlic purée or 1 teaspoon garlic, minced
2 teaspoons shallot, finely chopped
1/3 cup dry white wine
1 cup heavy cream
Kosher salt
Black pepper, freshly ground
1/4 cup parsley leaves, roughly chopped

Method

Prepare the hollandaise sauce. Set it aside.

Put the snails in a stainless steel skillet with the garlic purée, shallots, and wine. Place on a medium-high heat, and cook until the liquid is almost gone and you can begin to see the garlic and the shallots are beginning to sauté on the bottom of the pan.

Add the cream and bring to a rapid simmer. Let it simmer and reduce for about 3 minutes or until it begins to thicken.

Add salt and stir well.

Remove from heat and quickly stir in the hollandaise sauce. Grind black pepper over the mixture, and stir in the parsley.

Serve on very warm plates, accompanied by warm crusty French or Italian bread.

Yield: Four servings

Parboiled Sautéed Potatoes

12–15 tiny new potatoes
Olive oil
3   tablespoons kosher salt
2   tablespoons parsley, chopped

Method

Wash and rinse the potatoes well.

Put potatoes into 2 quarts salted boiling water. Lower the heat, and boil gently until tender, about 8 minutes. Run under cold water to cool. Drain.

Heat the oil in a skillet. Split the potatoes in half and place them cut side down in the skillet. Cook over medium heat for 6–8 minutes, or until the cut side is golden brown. Sprinkle with salt and parsley.

Yield: Four servings

Variations

- Three to four minutes before sautéeing is finished, add as many cloves of unpeeled garlic as you wish. Sprinkle liberally with kosher salt, rosemary, or any other fresh herb.
- Sprinkle with 1/4 cup hot, freshly sautéed, double-smoked bacon bits.
- Sprinkle cooked potatoes with 1/4 cup chopped scallion tops.
- Sauté potatoes in unsalted butter instead of oil. Add basil or oregano and sprinkle with finely grated Parmesan cheese.

Herb Toast

Note: "Amuses gueules," or mouth tickling, is a French idiomatic expression for a variety of little appetizers. They serve the same purpose as an apéritif—to stimulate. They are usually simple and are never designed to satisfy the appetite, only to open it up or act as a prelude. These herb toasts are simple to prepare and taste delicious.

8 tablespoons unsalted butter, room temperature
1 tablespoon garlic purée
1 pinch kosher salt
1/4 teaspoon ground black pepper
2 tablespoons fresh herbs, such as thyme or tarragon
French or Italian bread

Method

Blend butter with garlic purée, adding salt, pepper, and the herbs of your choice. Spread on 1/4-inch-thick slices of French or Italian bread. Bake on a cookie sheet at 350° F. for 10–15 minutes, until the edges are slightly brown and the toasts become fragrant.

Yield: Four servings

Variations

- Sprinkle with grated grana, mozzarella, Gouda, Fontina, or Gruyère cheese.
- Add 1/4-inch-thick slices of tomato on top of the herbed butter.
- Sprinkle capers on top of the herbed butter.
- Dot the herbed butter with fine-quality pitted black olives.
- Dot the herbed butter with chopped sun-dried tomatoes.
- Sprinkle either herbed butter, or the cheese variation, with sautéed double-smoked bacon bits.

Pizza Turnovers

Pizza crust (see page 45)
12   Italian-type sausages, hot or sweet
1   cup onions, finely diced
3   tablespoons olive oil
1   teaspoon kosher salt
1/2 teaspoon black pepper, freshly ground
1   pinch fennel seed
1/4 cup coarsely ground cornmeal

Method

For manageability, roll out approximately one-half of the dough at a time on a well-floured board. Cut squares of dough to fit the length of the sausage. Allow the dough to rest while you prepare the remaining ingredients.

Melt onions in 2 tablespoons of olive oil, with salt, pepper, and fennel seed. Butterfly the sausages and gently sauté them in 1 tablespoon olive oil until they are lightly brown on both sides.

Place an equal amount of onion mixture on each square of dough. Place a butterflied sausage on top of the onions with the ends of the sausage pointing toward you. Fold the left side of the dough halfway over the sausage, making sure that the ends of the sausage hang slightly over the dough. Brush the edge of the dough with water. Fold the other side over and press gently to seal.

Place the turnovers on a cookie sheet that has been liberally sprinkled with cornmeal. Bake in a 425° F. oven for approximately 12 minutes, until they are lightly puffed and golden brown.

Yield: 12 turnovers

Bouillabaisse

For over twenty years I have had the pleasure of experiencing bouillabaisse, *la bouillabaisse, la vrai bouillabaisse.* There is as much disagreement on the ingredients of true bouillabaisse as there is on any controversial dish. I have developed a bouillabaisse that is truly delicious, but not overly complex, using fish that can be found relatively easily anywhere in the United States. The fish used in Marseilles, home of *la vrai bouillabaisse,* are available in New York, but their perishability makes them extremely expensive, and they are not generally available throughout the United States. Most important is the freshness of the fish.

Rouille is absolutely basic to the enhancement of bouillabaisse, and is frequently served in a mortar and passed from person to person to add to their bouillabaisse. Traditionally the rouille is made with sea urchin; however, for the purposes of this preparation we are presenting a simpler version.

My New York bouillabaisse also includes shellfish, not a part of *la vrai bouillabaisse,* but they produce what I feel is a truly wonderful blend of tastes and textures.

Ingredients for the Broth
- 2 leeks, finely chopped
- 1 tablespoon garlic purée or 3 cloves garlic, chopped
- 1/2 large onion, finely chopped
- 1/2 cup olive oil
- 1 quart fish fumet (see page 202)
- 1/2 teaspoon crushed fennel seed, or 1/2 bulb fresh fennel (if fresh fennel is available), chopped, and 1/2 teaspoon crushed fennel seed
- 2 bay leaves
- 10 black peppercorns
- 3 sprigs fresh thyme or 1/4 teaspoon dried thyme

  3 fresh tomatoes, peeled, seeded, and chopped, or 4 canned Italian-style tomatoes, chopped
2-inch piece orange rind
1 cup dry white wine
1 large pinch saffron
Kosher salt

Method

  In a stainless steel or porcelain pot, sauté the leeks, garlic, and onions in oil very slowly for 15 to 20 minutes, or until they are completely wilted.

  In a separate pot bring the fumet to a boil, then reduce to a moderate simmer. Add the wilted vegetables and their cooking juices to the fumet. Add the herbs, spices, tomatoes, and orange rind, then simmer for about 40 minutes.

  Strain, pressing down on the solid matter to make sure that you extract all the juices.

  Return the broth to the pot and add the wine and saffron. Bring to a medium simmer and reduce to about 7 cups.

  Taste for salt. The seafood that will be added to the bouillabaisse has some natural salt in it, so make sure you do not oversalt the broth. At this point the soup can be served as a *soupe de poissons,* with a garlic croûton.

Ingredients for the Rouille

  1 cup broth (prepare in advance)
  1 medium boiling potato, peeled and roughly chopped
  1 tablespoon garlic purée or 2 cloves garlic, finely chopped
  1 pimento, canned or bottled, chopped
  1/4 teaspoon crushed red pepper or 1/2 teaspoon ground chili pepper

Method

  Place the fully seasoned broth in a stainless steel saucepan and add the potato. Cook at a gentle simmer until the potato is completely soft, about 12–15 minutes. If the liquid cooks down too much, add 1/4 cup water. There should be some liquid left when the potato is cooked.

Allow the potato to cool slightly, then place it in a food processor or foodmill with garlic, pimento, and the red pepper flakes or chili pepper. Purée well. The sauce should be redolent of garlic and very peppery.

Ingredients for the Fish
- 12 small cherrystone clams, well washed
- 18 mussels, scrubbed
- One 2-pound lobster, quartered
- 8 shrimp, cleaned, split, and deveined
- 1/2 pound striped bass, cut into 1 1/2-inch slices
- 1/2 pound red snapper, cut into 1 1/2-inch slices
- 1 small pinch saffron
- Pernod or good-quality Bordeaux wine
- Parsley, roughly chopped

Scale and debone the fish. Using a tweezer or other fine instrument, make sure that all fine bones have been removed. (Halibut, sea bass, monk fish, or if nothing else is available, filet of sole can be be substituted.)

Method
Bring broth to a rolling boil in a large pot. Drop in the clams. Cook for 2 minutes. Add the mussels and cook 2 minutes more. Add the lobster and cook for another 2 minutes. Add the fish slices and the saffron. Cook for 5 minutes. Add shrimp during the final two minutes.

Turn off the heat and remove the fish and shellfish with a slotted spoon, dividing them proportionately among the serving plates. Check the broth and adjust the seasoning, if necessary. Ladle the hot broth over the fish. Add a splash of Pernod or Bordeaux. (This adds a note that brings out all of the tastes.) Sprinkle liberally with parsley and pass the rouille.

When you serve the soup, pass the rouille, and gently stir it through the broth. The potato in the rouille will slightly thicken the broth.

Make sure that you serve a side plate for each person to easily dispose of the shells from the bouillabaisse.
Serve with lots of hot garlic bread.

Yield: Four servings

Chapter IV

Cold Pork Salad with Cucumbers and Sesame Noodles

Dialogue

...the nature of things

Certain ingredients suggest themselves when you walk into the market. Understanding the nature of a particular ingredient assures its proper preparation and the choice of complementary flavors. This requires understanding the moisture, density, and inherent taste qualities of a certain food so you can enhance and adjust. Scallops seize and cook within seconds. Shrimp take a few more seconds. In a dish in which both are cooked together, each must be added at a different time, even though we are often talking in terms of split-second timing.

I strongly encourage you to experiment. Don't consider only the finished product. Consider the process. Feel free to experiment and learn about ingredients. If you start out with good ingredients, you know that the final result will be good, even if it is not completely successful.

When you taste things during the cooking process, do not make up your mind right away. There will be a first taste, then the other aspects of taste will begin to emerge, seconds or minutes after. For instance, shellfish has its own intrinsic salt, so a preparation which calls for salt must not be seasoned before the effect of the shellfish is known.

Sometimes the order in which things are combined changes their taste. For example, when garlic and parsley are literally chopped together, the parsley cuts the acridness of the garlic because the juices are blended. Lemon or vinegar produces an acid reaction, as well as giving flavor. Richness often needs to be counterbalanced; a whipped cream, rich in and of itself, acts as a foil for a rich dessert like pecan pie. The addition of a small amount of coffee to chocolate can give depth to the chocolate without actually flavoring it. Knowledge of these tastes, and the way their properties react with one another, makes it possible to conceive and develop dishes.

Butter and cream function as agents upon which tastes are suspended. By understanding their effect in a sauce, you will understand whether you should reduce the flavoring agent in order to intensify the flavor before adding butter as a clear agent, or cream as a suspending agent.

Filet of Beef with Oriental Black Beans and Sweet Peppers

Oriental black beans, ginger, and sweet peppers create an environment that is most "untraditional" for filets of beef. Untraditional and yet absolutely right. . . . The beef has a taste and texture that is in no way cowed by the other ingredients.

- 2 tablespoons fermented black beans
- 4 beef filets, 6–7 ounces each
- 3 tablespoons soy oil
- 4 thin slices fresh ginger root
- 1 teaspoon garlic purée or 1 clove garlic, finely chopped
- 1 medium onion, thinly sliced
- 1 large sweet red pepper, seeded, membranes removed, chopped into 1/2-inch squares
- 1 cup beef-veal stock (see page 203)
- 3 tablespoons dry sherry
- 1 1/2 teaspoons soy sauce
- 2 tablespoons cold unsalted butter
- 1 package Oriental buckwheat noodles
- 1/2 cup snow peas, stem ends nipped and strings pulled down
- 1/4 cup water

Method

Soak the black beans in warm water to cover for 10 minutes.

Pan-broil or sauté the filets to the desired degree of doneness. Remove the filets from the heat and set aside to rest while preparing the sauce.

Drain and mash the black beans with a fork. Set aside.

In a heavy-bottomed stainless steel skillet, heat 2 tablespoons oil until hot. Stir in the ginger and garlic. Cook for 1 minute, but do not brown. Add the onion and sweet pepper. Lower the heat, cover, and cook for 8–10 minutes.

Add the mashed black bean purée and stock. Bring to a boil and cook for 5 minutes.

Add sherry, soy sauce, and any juices that have been released from the cooked filets. Cook for an additional 2–3 minutes. Permit the sauce to reduce and monter au beurre.

Place the filets into a 400° F. oven for 3–4 minutes, to warm them through. Meanwhile, prepare the noodles according to package directions. Toss the snow peas in 1 tablespoon hot oil for about 35 seconds. Splash with the water and toss for 45 seconds. Sprinkle with salt to taste. Serve the filets on beds of noodles with the sauce spooned over.

Arrange the snow peas on the plates with the beef.

Yield: Four servings

Frozen Espresso with Chocolate Curls and Cream

The blend of strong coffee, cream, and chocolate has universal appeal. This dessert takes these tastes and produces a new, simple variation.

1 1/2 teaspoons soy sauce
2 tablespoons cold unsalted butter
Sugar to taste
2 tablespoons Kahlua or creme de cacao
1 cup heavy cream, lightly whipped
2 teaspoons shaved semi-sweet or bittersweet chocolate

Method

Brew an espresso infusion. Add the water, then sweeten to taste. The mixture will be slightly less sweet when very cold. Pour the liquid into an ice cube tray and freeze until solid.

Put the espresso ice cubes into a food processor. Add the Kahlua or creme de cacao and purée.

Spoon into serving glasses and top with lightly whipped cream and shaved chocolate. Chocolate can be easily shaved with a vegetable peeler.

(Note: The success of this recipe is dependent upon the use of a very powerful processor like a Robot Coupe™ or a Cuisinart™.)

Calves' Liver with Root Vegetables

- 2 tablespoons unsalted butter or oil
- 3 cups beef stock (see page 203)
- 1 cup onion, thinly sliced
- 12 tiny Belgian carrots, peeled
- 2 leeks, white part only, well washed and coarsely chopped
- 1 celery root knob, peeled and cut into 1/2-inch cubes
- 1 3/4 pounds calves' liver (in one piece)
- 2 tablespoons soy oil
- 1/2 teaspoon sugar
- 1 large pinch kosher salt
- 3 tablespoons sherry wine vinegar
- 2 tablespoons cold unsalted butter, cut into pieces
- 1 tablespoon chives, chopped

Method

Cook the onion in butter or oil until well colored. Add the stock and gently simmer for 30 minutes. Strain, and return the stock to the stove. Continue cooking until reduced by half. Set aside.

Cook the carrots in salted water until just tender; cool in cold water. Cook the leeks in lightly salted water for 10–12 minutes; drain well. Cook the celery root in salted water until just tender; cool in cold water.

Lightly oil the liver. Place it on a rack set in a roasting pan. Bake in a preheated 400° F. oven for 20–25 minutes. Test by touching the liver in the center: there should be a resistance, but it should not be too solid (unless you prefer your liver more than medium rare). Firmness designates the degree of doneness. Remove from oven and let rest.

While the liver is baking, put sugar, salt, and sherry wine vinegar into a noncorrosive pan and bring to a simmer. Add the beef stock and bring to a boil. Cook for about 8–10 minutes, or until it is reduced to approximately 1 cup.

Add the vegetables and cook for 2 minutes to heat through. Remove pan from heat. Carve the liver into slices and arrange on heated plates, with the vegetables around it. Return sauce to the heat and gently swirl in the cold butter. Taste for salt and add as necessary.

Spoon sauce over, and sprinkle with chives.

Yield: Four servings

Potato Salad with Garlic, Grana, and Double-Smoked Bacon

Potatoes can stand on their own or accept an infinite variety of complementary tastes. This potato salad combines the smokiness of double-smoked bacon, the richness of a well-aged grana, and the magical quality of garlic.

- 1/4 cup double-smoked bacon, finely diced
- 2 tablespoons olive oil
- 1 1/2 pounds small new potatoes, washed and halved
- 1/2 cup lemon mayonnaise (see page 208)
- 1/4 cup grana, coarsely grated
- 1/4 cup flat (Italian) parsley, roughly chopped
- 1 teaspoon garlic purée
- Kosher salt
- Black pepper, coarsely ground

Method

Sauté the bacon in oil until lightly browned.

Cook the potatoes in 3 quarts of rapidly boiling salted water for approximately 15 minutes, or until fork-tender but not too soft. Remove from the heat, cool rapidly by pouring cold water over the potatoes, and drain well.

Put the mayonnaise and potatoes in a bowl and add grana, bacon bits, parsley, and garlic purée. Toss well. Add salt and pepper to taste.

Yield: Four servings

Variation

- Remove 1/4 pound of fine Italian sausage from its casing and brown lightly in olive oil. Make sure it does not become crisp. Drain, and add in place of the bacon.

Cold Pork Salad with Cucumbers and Sesame Noodles

The "hot" of the sesame oil is balanced by the "cold" of the cucumber, while the cumin, mustard, and soy add another note to this salad.

Sauce Ingredients

- 1 leek, white part only, washed and finely cut
- 3 tablespoons soy sauce
- 1 tablespoon hot sesame oil
- 1 tablespoon grainy mustard
- 1 tablespoon honey cup prepared mustard, or 1 tablespoon Dijon-type mustard mixed with 1 tablespoon honey
- 1/4 cup water
- 1 tablespoon garlic purée or 2 cloves garlic, finely chopped
- 1 teaspoon ground cumin
- 1 pound loin of pork (Roast the pork to an internal temperature of 190°. Let it cool. Leftover loin of pork can also be used.)
- 1 package Oriental buckwheat noodles
- 1 cucumber

Method

Prepare the buckwheat noodles so that they are al dente. Cool under cold running water, then drain well.

Put all of the sauce ingredients into a bowl and combine well.

Peel the cucumber. Use the peeler to shave the cucumber lengthwise down to the seeds on all sides. Discard the seeds.

Thinly slice the pork.

Make a nest of buckwheat noodles and arrange cucumber shavings around the nest. Arrange pork slices in the nest. Drizzle sesame sauce on top and serve.

Yield: Four servings

Asparagus, Westphalian Ham, and Pasta with Chèvre Sauce

24–28 asparagus tips
1/2   pound pasta shells
1   shallot, chopped
2   tablespoons unsalted butter
1/2   cup Westphalian ham, diced
1/2   cup dry white wine
1   cup heavy cream
6   ounces Beurre de Chèvre, or another type of chèvre
3–4   grinds black pepper
Kosher salt

Method
　　Plunge the asparagus tips in boiling salted water for about 3 minutes, or until they are cooked through but still al dente. Rinse under cold water to cool. Set aside.
　　Cook the shells in boiling salted water. Drain well and rinse with cold water to stop the cooking. Set aside.
　　Gently cook the shallot until translucent in butter, then add and lightly sauté the Westphalian ham. Pour in the wine, and reduce to approximately 2 tablespoons of liquid. Over medium heat, add cream and Beurre de Chèvre. Stir rapidly, and simmer,

uncovered, until lightly thickened. Add pepper and salt to taste, and keep warm.

Plunge the shells into almost boiling water to warm them and drain well again. Add the asparagus tips to the chèvre sauce.

Place shells on each plate, divide the Westphalian ham and asparagus over the shells and spoon on the sauce.

Yield: Two servings (four as an appetizer)

Butter Cream Cake

6 eggs
1 pinch kosher salt
1/3 cup granulated sugar
1 1/2 cups ground almonds
2 tablespoons flour
4 ounces unsalted butter, clarified
1/8 teaspoon almond extract

Method

Butter two 8-inch springform pans. Line the bottoms with waxed paper or baking parchment, then butter the paper and flour the entire pan, shaking out excess flour.

Preheat the oven to 350° F.

Break the eggs into a mixing bowl. Warm the eggs by lowering the bowl into a bowl of hot tap water. Mix the eggs well. Beat the eggs with salt at medium speed until they gain volume. Still beating, slowly add the sugar. Beat at high speed until the eggs have tripled in volume.

Sprinkle one-third of the nuts over the eggs and fold in. Repeat until all the nuts are added. Fold the butter into the mixture, half at a time. Sprinkle on the flour and fold into the mixture. Add the almond extract and fold.

Divide the batter between the pans. Bake for 20–25 minutes, until the edges are golden. Remove and cool on a rack.

Turn the cakes out and trim the edges, brushing away loose particles. Allow to cool completely before icing.

Butter Cream Icing

    1/3   cup, plus 1 tablespoon granulated sugar
    1/4   cup water
    1   teaspoon white vinegar
    3   egg whites
    1   cup unsalted butter, at room temperature

Method

Combine the 1/3 cup sugar, water, and vinegar in a stainless steel saucepan. Stir over low heat until the sugar is completely dissolved. Increase the heat and boil until the bubbles become small and numerous. When the mixture begins to look syrupy, remove from the heat.

Beat the egg whites in a very clean bowl until they begin to form soft peaks. Gradually beat the 1 tablespoon sugar into the egg whites. When they become firm, quickly bring the sugar syrup back to a simmer. In a fine stream, while constantly beating, add the syrup to the egg whites. After all has been incorporated, continue beating until it cools.

Cream the butter until it is soft and fluffy. With a wire whisk, beat 1 dollop of butter at a time into the icing.

Yield: 2 cups

Variations

- Mocha: add 5 ounces semi-sweet chocolate, 4 tablespoons espresso coffee, and 2 tablespoons cognac.
- Add 2–3 tablespoons Grand Marnier and 1 teaspoon grated orange rind.
- Add 1 cup ground macadamia nuts soaked for 5 minutes in fine rum.

- Add 1 cup ground hazelnuts soaked in 1 tablespoon Fra Angelica.
- Add 3 tablespoons Bailey's Irish Cream.
- Add 1/4 cup puréed strawberries or raspberries.
- Add 1/4 cup fresh lemon juice and 1 teaspoon finely grated lemon rind.
- Add 5 ounces bittersweet chocolate or 2 1/2 ounces bitter plus 2 1/2 ounces bittersweet chocolate, or 5 tablespoons dark imported cocoa.

Wild Rice Salad

The nutty taste of the rice is countered by the sharp quality of the scallion, then the peppers add sweetness, crunch, and color to balance the vinegar in the dressing.

```
1     cup wild rice
1/3   cup olive oil
1     teaspoon kosher salt
3     teaspoons red wine vinegar or sherry wine vinegar
1/2   cup scallions, diced
1/4   cup sweet red pepper, diced
1/4   cup green pepper, diced
1/4   cup parsley, roughly chopped
1/4   cup raw carrots, finely diced
Optional: 1/2 cup orange sections, membranes
   removed
```

Method

Prepare the wild rice according to the recipe on page 215, but omit the butter. Cool the rice. (To speed the cooling, you can spread it out on a flat pan in a thin layer.) Put the rice in a bowl and toss with olive oil. Add the salt and toss again. Add wine vinegar and toss again. Add the scallions, peppers, parsley, carrots, and orange sections, if desired. Toss well. Check for seasoning.

Yield: Four servings

Scrambled Eggs on Gravlax

The hollandaise sauce in conjunction with the dilled salmon adds a new dimension to the American classic, eggs Benedict.

  Hollandaise sauce (see page 207)
- 8 eggs, at room temperature
- 1 teaspoon kosher salt
- 1/4 cup half-and-half or heavy cream
- 2 tablespoons unsalted butter
- 4 English muffins, split, toasted, and buttered while warm
- 6 ounces Gravlax or Scottish, Irish, or Faroe Island smoked salmon, sliced very thin
- 1 tablespoon chopped chives or 1/4 teaspoon dill, freshly chopped

  Black pepper, coarsely ground

Method

Scrambled Eggs

Prepare the hollandaise sauce and set it aside to keep warm.

Break the eggs into a mixing bowl. Add salt and cream. With a fork gently break and mix with side-to-side strokes till the eggs are just combined. *Do not beat:* less mixing is better. The mixture should not be all one color. The result should be a multi-textured egg.

Gently cook the eggs in the butter in a medium-size frying pan over medium to low heat. With a wooden spoon or a rubber spatula, keep the eggs constantly moving, being sure to lift the cooked eggs off the bottom of the pan. One minute before the desired texture is reached, remove the pan from the heat and add 2 generous tablespoons of hollandaise sauce. Gently stir through. The residual heat will continue to cook the eggs to the desired doneness.

Spoon each portion of eggs on top of warm English muffins that have been covered with slices of Gravlax. Sauce with the hollandaise. Sprinkle with chives or dill and grind pepper to taste.

Yield: Four servings

Variation

- Poach 2 eggs per person in place of the scrambled eggs. Proceed as above.

Stuffed Potatoes

The ingredients here are given for a single serving.

Stuffed potatoes have the flexibility to change character with ingredients, and there are any number of herbs that can help alone or in concert with cheese, sour cream, or bacon.

1 Idaho potato, washed
Olive oil or butter
1 tablespoon double-smoked or other bacon, diced
1 pinch kosher salt
Black pepper, freshly ground
1 teaspoon unsalted butter, melted
2 1/2 tablespoons sour cream
 ¼ sprig fresh thyme, leaves removed, or fresh chives or fresh tarragon, plus extra sprigs for serving

Method

 Lightly oil the potato with olive oil or butter and pierce the skin on top to vent. Bake at 425° F. for approximately 50 minutes, until tender when pierced with a fork.

 Sauté the bacon and keep it warm.

 After baking, cut off a lid about 1/2 inch down from the top of the potato. Reserve the lid. With a spoon, carefully carve out the flesh and place it in a mixing bowl, leaving a shell 1/4–1/2-inch thick.

 While the potato pulp is still hot, stir in the bacon. Add salt, pepper, butter, sour cream, and thyme or chives, or tarragon. Stir well and spoon the hot mixture back into the skin.

 Return the potato and the lid to the hot oven for about 2 minutes, to make sure that it is piping hot.

 Place a sprig of fresh thyme, 3 sprigs of chives, or a sprig of tarragon (depending upon which was used during the preparation) on top of the potato, and replace the lid. Serve.

Red Snapper in an Aromatic Broth with Vegetables and Ginger Hollandaise

The clear broth is Oriental in origin and the rich ginger hollandaise adds a western accent to red snapper.

- 1 cup hollandaise sauce (see page 207)
- 1 1/2-inch piece of fresh ginger
- 4 filets red snapper, 6–7 ounces each, skin on, all bones removed
- 3 cups fish fumet (see page 202)
- 1/4 cup dry white wine
- 1 leek, white part only, washed and julienned
- 2 medium tomatoes, peeled, seeded, and chopped, or 3 Italian-style canned tomatoes, chopped
- 1 tablespoon shallot, chopped
- Optional: Six 1/4-inch-thick slices of lotus root, peeled and cut in half
- 9 small whole or 4 large slices shiitake mushrooms, fresh or dried and reconstituted or any Oriental-style mushroom
- 1/2 cup carrots, julienned
- 1/2 pound fresh spinach leaves, well washed and roughly chopped
- 1/4 cup reconstituted Japanese Hijiki seaweed
- 12 fresh snow peas, strings removed
- Kosher salt
- 24 whole flat parsley leaves

Method

Prepare the hollandaise in advance and keep it warm. Grate the fresh ginger into a bowl, catching both the ginger and the liquid. Take the grated ginger in your hand and squeeze the liquid into the hollandaise. Discard the pulp. If the ginger does not yield 3/4–1 teaspoon liquid, grate enough extra to produce that amount of liquid. Taste to see if the ginger flavor is pronounced enough.

Clean, peel, and chop all of the vegetables before beginning the poaching of the fish (see page 214).

In a deep stainless steel skillet, in 1 1/2 cups of the fumet and the white wine, gently poach the fish. Remove the fish to a side plate.

Strain the poaching liquid into a clean pot and add the rest of the fumet. Raise the heat and reduce for 5 minutes.

Add the leek, tomatoes, shallot, and lotus root if desired. Cook for about 3 minutes at a rolling simmer.

Add the seaweed and snow peas. Cook for approximately 2 minutes. Season the broth to taste with salt.

Place one filet, skin side up, in an individual heated serving bowl. Bowls should be used because the liquid is a broth and needs to be contained. Distribute the vegetables around, not on, the fish. Ladle about 3/4 cup of broth per person over the fish and vegetables. Spoon the ginger hollandaise on the fish, allowing some of the skin to show through. The sauce will drizzle down into the broth. Float whole leaves of parsley in each bowl.

Yield: Four servings

Variation

- Substitute 4 turbot filets for the red snapper.

Chapter V

Red Snapper in Red Wine Sauce

Heightening

...bringing food up to taste

To bring out the essence and perfumes of food, and to enhance the flavors, herbs, spices, and other ingredients such as butter and wine are used. It is a contrived action in the most positive sense.

"Watching the food" is an extremely important aspect of the preparation. It implies a total involvement on the part of the cook, because there are exact moments when the proper result is reached. One does not taste for the element that one is adding but tastes to discover if the addition or application has brought out the correct balance of all the ingredients. Many people think that a herb or spice is something that rests on top of the other tastes, as opposed to bringing to life all the other tastes. "Heightening" is bringing forth a taste. It is almost like an optical illusion! As in the use of complementary colors in painting, you can bring forth a flavor by placing another near it. For instance, in order to heighten the natural sweetness of lobster, the juxtaposition of a cream and Sauterne sauce creates the illusion of a greater natural sweetness in the lobster.

Clearly, salt is one of the most important elements in heightening. When I taste, it is not for the salty quality but rather to see if all the elements have been thrust forward enough so that the balance of the flavors is satisfying to one's taste, and correct in their natural balance. During the past few years, there has been a hysteria in the United States over salt. It is very important that those people who are on salt-restricted diets find other ways of heightening their food. However, salt in and of itself, when used properly, is not something that should be avoided. Frequently people salt to "create" a taste, as opposed to bringing other tastes out. You should strive to bring your own taste buds back into alignment, and let that dictate when the proper balances are made.

In food, as in art, there are certain objective judgments as to what is good and what is bad. There are also subjective judgments, based upon one's personal taste. In writing this cookbook, I have discovered that it's extraordinarily difficult to try to explain in words alone any important aspect of cooking, such as the importance of salt. A preparation requires a certain amount of salt for heightening, but each individual responds to salt differently. This variation is based upon the tastes that we have developed over years, and our taste buds' sensitivities, influenced by our own physical make-up.

There are specific times to add ingredients, to maximize their effect in the cooking process. Those specific times are frequently taken for granted, because out of habit we have been taught to add ingredients in a particular order. However, different cooking processes affect the taste of heightening elements. When black pepper is put into a preparation after cooking, it has one taste; but if it is put in too soon, it can become slightly bitter.

Fresh spices and herbs are becoming more widely available in the United States. All the recently popular American cuisines have sung the praises of these herbs and spices. Rosemary has a very different taste and texture when fresh. It is milder and yet deliciously insidious. Basil, thyme, tarragon, and sage all have major taste differences between fresh and dried. Working with fresh herbs adds to the wonder of cooking. It is relatively simple to grow herbs in your own garden or in small pots in a kitchen.

Butter lubricates, acts as a clear agent, adds volume, and also heightens. It can be used to make a sauce less intense or to give it added viscosity.

Wine, vinegar, and lemon are acids and are the piquant notes in a preparation. They give a point, or a thrust, lifting flavors off of your tongue. Condiments like capers, cornichons, and anchovies also add a piquant note and act as heightening agents.

Extracts insinuate an essence in a preparation. Whipped cream takes on a completely different character with the addition of vanilla, lemon, or orange extract. It is important to remember that extracts are extremely condensed preparations and must be used sparingly. The flavor should be subtle. Commercially baked preparations have a tendency to overindulge in the use of sugar and extracts, thus losing the intended flavor.

Sugar is a heightening element, but in savory preparations there are ways of producing sweetness with the use of naturally sweet elements, such as turnips, parsnips, carrots, and onions. When cooked slowly, they release a natural sweetness that heightens in more subtle and complementary ways than through the addition of sugar. When cooking liver, for instance, two heightening agents are generally used—the sweetening of onion and carrot and the piquancy of sherry vinegar.

In America, sugar is used to such a degree that it literally blocks out tastes. Most recipes are oversugared. You will find that with a little patience and experimentation, you can cut back a great deal on sugar, which will actually open up the other flavors in your preparations. When preparing a fruit tart, for instance, instead of adding a sweet custard as a base, I use a tart crème fraîche that has been lightly beaten with a fruit liqueur to a spreadable texture. The only sugar is in a light glaze on the fruit.

Your tongue will get back to normal after dispensing with the excessive use of sugar and salt in commercial preparations. The tastes may seem odd in the beginning, but with time, your tolerance for sugar will lessen, and your tastes will come back in line.

The most important thing to understand about heightening is balance—how one takes, interrelates, and opens up one taste into the next. If you remember that heightening is bringing food up to taste, you will begin to understand these subtle interrelationships.

Shoulder of Pork with Prosciutto and Green Peppercorns

The salt quality of the prosciutto with the young green taste of pepper works with the unctuosity of the shoulder cut of pork.

1	small pork shoulder, boned and butterflied by the butcher
1/4	cup grainy mustard
1/4	pound thinly sliced prosciutto
2	tablespoons green peppercorns
2	tablespoons olive oil
2	cups dry white wine
1	cup water
2	onions, roughly chopped
2	carrots, roughly chopped
2	bay leaves
10	black peppercorns
1	tablespoon garlic purée or 2 cloves garlic, chopped

Method

Lay the shoulder out with the skin side down. Liberally spread with the mustard, and cover the entire surface with slices of prosciutto. Sprinkle green peppercorns over the prosciutto, and roll into a neat bundle. Tie in several places so that it will hold its shape while cooking.

In a heavy-bottomed stainless steel skillet, heat oil until it is almost smoking. Lower heat and brown the shoulder on all sides until golden. Place the meat in a casserole that is just large enough to hold it. Make sure the casserole has a tight-fitting cover. Add wine, water, onions, carrots, bay leaves, black peppercorns, and garlic. Bring to a gentle simmer on top of the stove.

Cover, and place in a pre-heated 350° F. oven. Braise approximately 1 1/2 hours or until a meat thermometer registers 185° F. Check the liquid occasionally to be sure that it is only at a gentle simmer.

Remove the roast from the pan. Strain the liquid into a saucepan. Bring to a simmer and skim off the excess fat. Reduce by about half.

Taste for seasoning, adding salt if necessary.

Place slices of meat on a warm plate and moisten with juices.

Yield: Four servings

Snow Peas with Fresh Mint and Shallots

32–40   snow peas
2   tablespoons unsalted butter
1   tablespoon shallot, finely chopped
1/4   cup water
1   large pinch kosher salt
1   small pinch black pepper, freshly ground
8–10   fresh mint leaves

Method

Break off the stems of the snow peas and pull off their strings.

On a high flame heat butter in a frying pan until it just begins to brown. Add the snow peas and toss well in the butter.

Add the shallots and stir. Allow the mixture to cook for another minute, constantly moving the snow peas so they do not brown.

Add water to the hot pan, taking care to avoid the steam that will rise immediately.

Sprinkle with salt and pepper and cover for 1 minute. The snow peas will steam slightly because of the addition of the water. The snow peas should be bright green and very crunchy when done.

Tear the mint leaves and add to the pan. Stir, and serve.

Yield: Four servings

Shell Steak with Three Peppers

- 4 shell steaks, 8–9 ounces each and about 1 inch thick
- 2 tablespoons Szechuan peppercorns
- 2 tablespoons black peppercorns
- 2 tablespoons olive oil
- 1 tablespoon unsalted butter, plus 2 tablespoons unsalted cold butter
- 1 teaspoon garlic purée
- 1/2 teaspoon shallot, finely chopped
- 1/4 cup cognac
- 1/2 cup red wine
- 1/2 cup glace de viande (see page 204)
- 2 tablespoons green peppercorns, crushed
- 1 teaspoon kosher salt
- 2 tablespoons flat parsley leaves, roughly chopped

Method

Have the butcher remove the steak from the bones and trim the meat well.

Crush the Szechuan and black peppercorns with the flat side of a knife on a hard surface. Sprinkle the crushed pepper generously over both sides of each piece of meat. Then, using the heel of your hand, press the cracked pepper into the steaks.

Heat the oil and 1 tablespoon butter in a heavy-bottomed stainless steel skillet until it is almost smoking. Place the steaks in the pan and lower the heat to medium. Sauté the steaks to the desired doneness, making sure that they are mahogany brown on each side. Remove the steaks from the pan and place them on a plate on an angle, so the surfaces of the steaks do not lie flat against the plate.

Continue to use the oil in the pan unless it has been burned. If it has, discard it and add 1 tablespoon olive oil. Place the shallots and garlic in the oil and cook at a medium-low heat for 3–4 minutes. Remove pan from heat. Pour in the cognac, away from open flame. Put the pan back on the heat cautiously, as it will ignite. Cover the pan quickly to douse the flame, then add the wine. Swirl the contents of the pan and gently dislodge the browned ingredients from the bottom. Cook to reduce the liquid by two-thirds.

Add glace de viande, the exuded juices from the steaks, and the green peppercorns. Cook for 4–5 minutes, until the sauce begins to thicken. Taste for salt.

Remove from the heat and monter au beurre.

Place the steaks on warm plates and spoon the sauce over. Sprinkle with parsley.

Yield: Four servings

Steak Tartare

The piquancy of the Pick-A-Peppa sauce and cornichons add the necessary accent to the raw taste of the beef.

- 1 pound filet of beef
- 1 egg yolk
- 1 teaspoon kosher salt
- 1/2 teaspoon black pepper, freshly ground
- 1 teaspoon Worcestershire or Pick-A-Peppa sauce, or 1/2 teaspoon of each
- 1 clove garlic, finely chopped
- 4 cornichons, finely chopped
- 1 shallot, finely chopped

Optional: 4 anchovy filets, mashed with a fork

Fresh parsley, chopped

Method

Trim away all gristle and fat from the meat. With the blade of a sharp knife held perpendicular to the meat, but aligned with the grain, scrape the meat back and forth, making a purée. Continue to remove the gristle and fat as it surfaces. (Or place the meat, roughly chopped, in a food processor with a chopping blade, and finely chop in pulses for about 1 minute.)

Place the meat, egg yolk, salt, pepper, Worcestershire or Pick-A-Peppa sauce, and garlic in a bowl. Blend well. Serve with the condiments arranged on each plate.

This dish can also be served with the meat beautifully mounded on a serving plate; press half an eggshell into the center, place the yolk in the shell. Arrange the condiments around the meat in little piles, then mix at the table.

Chill the meat firm for about 1 hour, cut into 1/2-inch slices. Sprinkle with parsley and serve.

Yield: Four servings

Variation

- Take a long, thin loaf of Italian bread, cut off the ends, and cut into 6-inch lengths. Gently push out the doughy part of the bread with your fingers. Use your fingers to spread butter on the inside of the loaf, and pack with the steak tartare.

Pork Curry with Root Vegetables

This is a very delicate curry—one that can be enjoyed by people who are not curry lovers.

    One 8-chop center-cut loin of pork, boned and tied
    Freshly ground black pepper to taste
1   tablespoon olive or soy oil
1/2 cup chicken stock (see page 204)
1/2 cup dry white wine
2   carrots, peeled and chopped on the diagonal into 1/2-inch pieces
1   leek, white part only, well washed and roughly chopped
1   onion, cut into 8 pieces
1/4 teaspoon cumin seed, ground
1   teaspoon freshly ground curry powder
1   large pinch kosher salt
1/2 cup cream

Method

    Have butcher remove the eye of the chops from the bone, in one piece. Roll flap in and tie in several places. (Reserve the ribs and backbone, chopped in small pieces.)

    Rub the pork with ground black pepper. Place oil in stainless steel skillet and heat until just smoking. Place the pork and the bones in the skillet and brown well, turning often. While browning, the heat should be regulated so the fat does not burn.

    Add the stock, wine, and vegetables. Cover, and braise in 350° F. oven for about 1 1/2 hours, until an internal temperature of 190° registers on a meat thermometer. Discard bones, and remove the meat to a warm plate.

    Pour skillet ingredients into a food processor and purée with the chopping blade.

    Add cumin, curry powder, and salt to the puréed vegetables, and blend until completely combined. Pour the purée into a clean skillet and add cream. Bring these ingredients to heat and reduce until slightly thickened. Check for salt. Add generous grinds of black pepper.

Slice the pork thin. Make pools of curry sauce on each warm plate and place pork slices in the pools. Serve with Cucumber and Crème Fraîche Salad (see page 111) and Sour Cherry Compote (see page 150).

Yield: Four servings

Duck Livers with Sherry Wine Vinegar

For those who like liver this is a wonderful dish. The oaky, keglike taste of the sherry wine vinegar has an incisive effect on the smooth, rich quality of the liver.

- 2 duck livers
- 2 tablespoons oil, or 1 tablespoon butter plus 1 tablespoon oil
- 1 teaspoon shallot, finely chopped
- 3 tablespoons sherry wine vinegar
- 3/4 cup duck or chicken stock (see page 204)
- 3 tablespoons cold unsalted butter

Kosher salt
Black pepper, freshly ground
- 4 large lettuce leaves, chilled

Method

Sauté the livers in oil, or oil and butter, for about 2–3 minutes on each side. They should be pink in the middle.

Remove them from the pan and pour off any excess fat. Stir in the shallots and cook gently for 2–3 minutes.

Deglaze the pan with sherry wine vinegar. Add the stock and cook for 4–5 minutes and monter au beurre. Add salt to taste. Place thin slices of liver over lettuce leaves and spoon sauce over. Sprinkle liberally with black pepper.

Yield: Two appetizers

Note: I also like to serve this dish with one breast, and one confit leg, with a mound of wild rice with apricots and hazelnuts (see pages 104 and 35).

Belgian Carrots in Rosemary Butter

1 1/2   cups water
Two 3-inch sprigs fresh rosemary, or 1 teaspoon dried rosemary
1   teaspoon kosher salt
2   bags of tiny whole Belgian carrots
2   tablespoons unsalted butter
Black pepper, freshly ground

Method

Remove the tops of the carrots, then scrub them well with a brush or peel them. Very thick carrots should be split in half lengthwise so they are all of a similar thickness to ensure their arriving at the done point together.

Put the water and rosemary in a saucepan and bring to a boil. Add the salt and carrots. Cook at a rapid boil, uncovered. Test after 5 minutes. The carrots should be cooked but still have a bit of crunch to them. At this point there should only be about 1/2 inch of water in the pan. If there is more, pour off the excess.

Add the butter and return to a high heat, stirring gently. The high heat will cause the butter and water to reduce and thicken into a light glaze.

    Grind black pepper over the top and serve.

Yield: Four servings

Red Snapper in Red Wine Sauce

Ingredients for Filets

    Four 6-ounce filets of red snapper, fine bones carefully removed
- 1/4 cup glace de viande (see page 204)
- 1 tablespoon shallot, chopped
- 1/2 pound shiitake mushrooms, or other cultivated wild mushrooms, like oak mushrooms
- 3/4 cup sturdy red wine, such as an Italian Spana or a fine Bordeaux

    Kosher salt
    Black pepper, freshly ground
- 3 tablespoons unsalted butter

Poaching Ingredients
- 1/4 cup dry white wine
- 3/4 cup water
- 1 tablespoon shallot, chopped

Method

    Mix the wine, water, and shallots in a skillet. Poach the fish in this liquid in a skillet for 4–5 minutes (see page 214). If the fish is not cooked all the way through, don't be alarmed: it will cook further during the rest of the process. Remove the fish to a warm plate.

Pour out all but 1/2 cup of the poaching liquid. Add the glace de viande, shallots and mushrooms. Simmer until reduced by one-half. Add the wine and simmer for 7–8 minutes, until the liquid is slightly thickened and syrupy. Remove the skillet from heat. Taste for salt, and season as desired with salt and pepper.

Replace over low heat and swirl in the butter.

Place the filets on well-heated plates, and spoon sauce over.

Yield: Four servings

Veal Chops with Sun-Dried Tomatoes and Fontina Cheese

The nutlike quality of the sun-dried tomatoes and the oil in which they are soaked combined with the mellow buttery taste of the Fontina adds character to this neutral flavored meat.

  4 veal chops, about 1/2-inch thick
  Flour
  3 tablespoons olive oil
  1 1/2 ounces sun-dried tomatoes, chopped
  1 tablespoon shallot, chopped
  1/2 teaspoon black pepper, freshly ground
  16 fresh basil leaves, plus extra for the sauce
  Kosher salt
  4 ounces Fontina cheese, coarsely grated
  Tomato sauce (see page 210)

Method

Dust the veal chops with flour and tap off excess.

In a heavy-bottomed skillet, heat the olive oil almost to smoking, then add the veal chops. Turn heat down to medium-low. Cook 3–4 minutes until golden brown, then turn and cook for about 2 minutes.

Remove the chops to a heavy-bottomed baking pan, and place in a 425° F. oven for approximately 5 minutes. Remove the pan from oven and pack the top of each chop with an equal amount of tomatoes, shallots, black pepper, basil, and a pinch of salt. Cover completely with Fontina cheese. Return to the oven for approximately 4–5 minutes, until the cheese is melted. The veal chop will be pink at the bone.

Serve each chop on a pool of hot tomato sauce and float additional basil leaves in the sauce.

Yield: Four servings

Chapter VI

Sautéed Breast of Duck with Confit of Duck

Texture

...the final result

People frequently go blindly into a recipe without really ever knowing what the end result should look or taste like. They don't know if what they have prepared is correct or not. This chapter is designed to give you a clearer picture of what a dish should be. Texture is the tactile sense in the kitchen. At times, the joy of a preparation is the texture. The way a mousseline or a custard jiggles on the plate when it is perfectly prepared gives me great joy.

Balanchine, when teaching the Company, often used food analogies in his description of the way steps should be executed. There was a commonality that everyone could understand because of the sensuality that is present in both food and dance. For instance, "Mr. B" explained a dance step called a glissade, which is a moving from side to side, with an analogy to the quality of smoothness when with one stroke you spread soft butter over warm bread.

It is important for a cook to explore texture. It is necessary to touch the food when cooking. Someone once asked Balanchine what it was that made him decide when a young dancer was ready for large roles.

"Vell, you know iz like a potato.
You cook.
and cook.
and cook.

And tzen all of a sudden
. . . itz ready!"

Texture changes radically when an ingredient is cooked beyond its intended point. I use the word point in its traditional sense, meaning to the point of. . . . The correct words must be used to describe the proper texture.

Depend upon your own senses again. Even if you've never heard a melodic line before, it does not preclude your sensing when there is a missed note. Touch can tell you the state of doneness in a piece of meat without having to cut into it.

A restaurant chef certainly has the opportunity to touch, taste, and learn to gauge the doneness of a dish, because he prepares it over and over again. However, with some patience the home chef can do the same. At times the ingredients give visual cues. For example, when cooked over a flame, meat that has just cooked on one side to the point where it is warm but still pink in the middle will begin to exude pink juices on top. This is a cue to the cook to turn it. Obviously, if you want the meat cooked beyond pink, you continue to cook it. Anticipate the cue, if the meat is to be rare. A potato has a precise point at which it is done: the point at which a blade just easily pierces it. It is at that point—no point before, no point after—that it is properly cooked. Texture tells you when egg yolks and sugar have been beaten enough, because they make a ribbon. A Comice pear is ripe if it gives slightly when squeezed. I've frequently met people who have been exposed only to overcooked pasta or undercooked vegetables. For both foods, there is a point when the center has just lost its rawness, and from that point on the texture begins to change. Whether it be vegetables, pasta, or anything else, there is a state of doneness at a certain moment. Being able to judge and recognize that point is extremely important in freeing you from the technique of cooking, thus allowing the marvelous quality of spontaneity to light up your food.

Each element has its properly cooked stage. In a pesto sauce, pignoli nuts add both taste and texture. If they are added to the pesto too early, they become soft and lose their textural quality. In some dishes, like ratatouille, you want to completely intermingle the flavors and textures. You must never lose sight of the intention of the dish.

Heat, whether it be radiant or acid (vinegar, lime juice), changes the texture of things.

When you learn these principles, cooking becomes ever so much easier. You gain confidence when your fingers and mind become sensitized to the process. It is important to become aware of viscosity and density. Words tell you what to look for, but when words become generalized, they produce a generalized result. A misunderstanding of M. Fernand Point's Nouvelle Cuisine has produced vegetables that are basically warm but raw. In reality, a vegetable should be cooked to the point where it still has some crunch; the term in Chinese cuisine is "the sound that you hear in your ear when you chew."

Texture often makes the difference between something tasting right and taste being overwhelmed by a rubbery texture. A mousseline (mousse or mousseau, meaning airy) requires an airy quality, rather than a stiffened texture. Many kitchen machines are used improperly by people who don't understand the preparations. The food processor, which is an important addition to any kitchen, does not replace all other equipment. For a mousseline, or any other preparation that needs air, the processor should be used only to purée or chop the ingredients, then a whisk or a whisk-type mixer should be used to incorporate air into the preparation. That is the key element to the texture.

Odile Chocolate Cake

Odile, or the Black Swan, is a character in Tchaikovsky's *Swan Lake*. Over a twelve-year period I developed what I consider to be a chocoholic's dream. I finally introduced it for the first time at Sperry's Café in Saratoga Springs, New York. Recently "Stendahl on Food" named this "New York's Perfect Chocolate Cake." As you will see, there is no flour in it, and very little sugar. It is extraordinarily rich rather than sweet. (The better the quality of chocolate you use, the better the taste and texture of the cake.)

> 5 ounces bittersweet Belgian chocolate
> 2 ounces bitter Belgian chocolate
> 8 tablespoons unsalted butter, cut into pieces
> 3 eggs, separated
> 4 tablespoons sugar
> 3 tablespoons water
> 1/4 cup currants soaked in 1/4 cup Mandarin Napoleon Brandy or another orange-flavored liqueur
> 1/4 pound almonds, very finely chopped
> 1 pinch kosher salt
> Unsweetened whipped cream
> Green grapes

Method

Butter a 7- or 8-inch cake pan. Line the bottom with baking parchment or waxed paper. Butter the parchment and flour the entire pan, tapping out the excess.

Melt the chocolate and butter over, *not in*, gently simmering (never boiling) water.

Beat the egg yolks with the sugar until they turn light yellow and form a ribbon. In another bowl, beat the egg whites until they are stiff but not dry.

Combine the chocolate, beaten egg yolks, and water. Stir. Add the currants and liqueur. Add the ground almonds, and mix.

Stir in one-quarter of the egg whites, then lightly fold in the remaining egg whites.

Bake in a 325° F. oven. Check after 15 minutes. This cake cooks from the outside edge in. After about 20 minutes, when approximately 2 inches of the outer edge have cooked and risen, it is done. *Do Not Overcook!* Remove the cake from oven and allow it to cool. The inside texture should be slightly gooey, like a delicious candy. Therefore normal testing techniques are not appropriate.

Ingredients for Icing
- 3 ounces bittersweet Belgian chocolate
- 2 tablespoons unsalted butter, at room temperature

Method

Melt the chocolate over, *not in*, hot water. Remove it from the heat and slowly stir in butter, 1 tablespoon at a time. Continue to stir until the mixture has cooled to a spreading consistency.

Gently unmold the cooled cake, and spread icing over and around.

One fresh flower on the dark chocolate is very striking.

Note: Serve very small portions, with a small amount of unsweetened whipped cream and a few green grapes.

Smoked Tuna with White Beans

- 1 pound dry canellini or navy beans
- 1 tablespoon kosher salt
- 1/2–3/4 cup heavily garlic-infused mayonnaise (see page 208)
- 1 pound smoked tuna, or one 8-ounce can Italian tuna, well drained
- Black pepper, freshly ground
- Fresh parsley, chopped

Method

Pick over the beans carefully to remove any stones. Place them in a bowl, and add water to cover by 2 inches. Let soak overnight. A more rapid method is to put the beans into a saucepan, and add water to cover by 1 inch. Bring just to a boil, turn off the heat, and let sit for 1 hour.

Bring the beans up to a boil, and then simmer approximately 45 minutes. If the water level goes below the beans, add more water to cover. Cooked beans should be completely yielding, but not mushy. If they are not done after 45 minutes, continue to simmer but check often, as they cook rapidly after a certain point.

Remove from heat, drain, and rinse in cold water. Let cool.

When the beans are well drained and cold, add the salt and toss well. Add the garlic mayonnaise, tuna chunks, and pepper. Toss. Check for seasoning and sprinkle with parsley. Serve with hot garlic bread.

Yield: Four servings

Sabayon au Poire

If you have all the ingredients assembled, you can prepare this between courses in 4–5 minutes. It is a very elegant and delicious dessert, and will not take you away from your guests for too long.

    5   egg yolks
    1/4   cup sugar
    1/2   cup Eau de Vie Poire
    Optional: Fresh berries or other fruit

Method

Put the egg yolks and sugar in the top of a stainless steel double boiler. Beat until they turn pale yellow and form a ribbon. Add the Poire. Place over, *not in*, hot (never boiling) water. Continue to beat until the cooking of the eggs thickens the mixture. Some people like this preparation very thick; I prefer a consistency like a runny custard.

Spoon the sabayon into sherbet glasses, or use it as a warm sauce over fresh fruit. The sauce can also be served in a bowl with a beautifully arranged mound of berries to the side; each person dipping the berries in the sauce for themselves.

Variation

- Cook the mixture to a slightly thicker consistency. Remove it from the heat but continue to beat for 2 minutes, to remove the residual heat. Set aside to cool completely. Lightly whip 1 cup heavy cream until it forms soft peaks. Gently fold the cream into the cooled mixture. This variation can be served immediately or be covered, refrigerated, and served the next day.

Brie Italienne

The crunch of the crust and the warm gooeyness of the cheese are delicious counterbalances and produce hors d'oeuvres that are truly "finger lickin" good.

1/2-inch slices of a boule or a French or Italian bread
Unsalted butter, at room temperature
Garlic purée
Black pepper, freshly ground
Brie cheese

Method

Liberally spread the slices with butter, then with garlic purée. Sprinkle profusely with black pepper and cover with slices of brie. Place in a 450° F. oven until the cheese has melted and the bread is toasted, about 5–8 minutes. If served as a first course, slices can be floated in a pool of tomato sauce or lightly cooked spinach (see pages 210, 214).

Variations

- Prepare the slices without cheese. Sauté finely chopped shallot and spinach in a little bit of olive oil. Sprinkle with about 1 tablespoon of good sherry wine vinegar or red wine vinegar. Drain and put to the side, but keep warm. Toast the breads. While the toasts are still warm, place a nest of spinach on top of each toast, with one raw sparkling-fresh oyster in the center. Pass the peppermill.
- Cut a *ficelle* into 1-inch rounds. Spread the slices with butter and garlic purée and toast them in the oven. Place a ball of steak tartare (see page 87) on the top.
(A *ficelle* is a long thin loaf only about 1 1/2" thick.)

Sautéed Breast of Duck with Confit of Duck

This recipe involves many preparations. Confit was originally designed as a method of preserving over long periods of time without refrigeration. The duck confit will store in a refrigerator for 2 to 3 months. What is particularly interesting about this recipe is that it utilizes all the parts of the duck; there is absolutely no waste. The confit should be prepared two days—or more—before the sautéed breast of duck.

2   Long Island ducks

Ingredients for Stock
>   Roasted duck bones
>   Water to cover
>   1/2   onion, stuck with a clove
>   1   bay leaf
>   1   medium carrot, chopped
>   3   Allspice berries

Ingredients for Confit
>   (Prepare 48 hours in advance)
>   4   Duck legs
>   2   tablespoons kosher salt
>   2   bay leaves, 4 allspice berries, 6 sprigs fresh thyme, crushed together
>   Rendered duck fat
>   Additional animal fat to cover

Ingredients for Sauce
>   1   teaspoon shallot, chopped
>   1/4   cup red wine
>   3   cups duck stock
>   1   teaspoon sherry wine vinegar
>   Kosher salt to taste
>   2   tablespoons cold unsalted butter

Ingredients for Breasts
>   4   duck breasts
>   1   tablespoon duck fat

Preparation of Duck Stock

Remove the fatty flap by the neck area of each duck. Cut it off close to the body. Trim off the 2 pads of fat on the inside of the cavity openings. Place the fat into a pan for rendering.

Cut the wings off at the joint where they meet the body, and set aside. With the breast side up, make incisions on either side of the breastbone. Remove each breast. Then cut down against the body until you hit the leg socket. Hold the carcass with one hand and bend the leg and thigh down and under until the joint pops out. Cut the leg off at that joint. Repeat with the other leg. Remove the rest of the skin from the carcasses. Roughly chop the carcasses.

Place the carcasses and necks with the wings in a roasting pan and bake at 400° F. until they are brown.

Trim the excess fat from the breasts and the legs and place this fat in the rendering pot with the fat from the cavities.

Put the roasted necks, carcasses and wings in a stockpot. Cover with water and gently bring to a simmer. Skim off any excess fat and add the 1/2 onion with a whole clove inserted, bay leaf, small carrot, and allspice berries. Simmer for 4 hours and strain. Set aside.

To render the duck fat, add about 1/2 cup water to the fat. Place it over low heat and melt until almost all the solids have dissolved. Then strain through a cloth or coffee filter paper. Set aside.

Confit of Duck

Place the duck legs in a deep bowl. Crush together the bay leaves, allspice berries, and fresh thyme leaves, and sprinkle over the duck. Sprinkle with 2 tablespoons salt. Cover well, and refrigerate for 24–48 hours. Wipe the excess salt from the legs and submerge them in a skillet of rendered duck fat. If there is not enough fat to cover, you will have to add some more fat, such as lard or animal fat. Cook over very low flame for 1 1/2 hours, or until legs are fork-tender. Remove the skillet from the heat and let it cool. Place the legs in a ceramic or glass container. Strain the fat and pour it over the legs. Cool completely and refrigerate until needed. The legs can remain in the rendered fat, refrigerated, for several months.

For the Confit of the Legs

To use the duck legs, pull them out of the fat. Rinse under warm water to remove excess fat and dry. Broil about 8 minutes, turning once, until hot through and crusty.

They can be used in cassoulet or without broiling, cut into slivers and added to salads.

Duck Breasts

Place 1 tablespoon rendered duck fat in a skillet. Heat to almost smoking. After pricking the skin well, to permit excess fat to be released, place the breasts in the skillet, skin side down.

Lower the heat to medium. Cook for about 5 minutes on the skin side, until it turns a nice golden brown. Keep pouring off accumulating fat into a container. Turn over and cook 4–5 minutes, until breasts are slightly springy in the center. Remove to a dish.

If the fat has not burned, pour off all but about 1/2 teaspoon and sauté shallots in it for 2 minutes. Remove the skillet from the heat and add the red wine. Return it to the heat and let it cook down almost completely. Add duck stock. Turn to medium heat and reduce by half. Add the sherry wine vinegar and salt. Monter au beurre with cold butter.

Carve the duck breasts on an angle like London broil, very thin. Then fan out slices on heated plates and spoon the sauce over.

Yield: Four servings

Custard

2 1/2   cups milk
3   whole eggs
3   egg yolks
1/4   cup sugar
3   tablespoons Bailey's Irish Cream
1/2   cup currants, soaked in Mandarin Napoleon Brandy or other orange-flavored liqueur

Method

Bring the milk just to a simmer.

Beat the eggs and yolks with the sugar until pale yellow. While constantly beating, pour milk in a thin stream into the eggs. Mix well. Add the Bailey's Irish Cream.

Spread soaked currants evenly over the bottom of a 6-cup

glass baking dish or in individual custard cups. Pour in the custard. Place the dish in another dish large enough to bring water 3/4 of the way up the sides of the custard dish. Fill outside pan with hot water.

Bake in a 325–350° F. oven for 35–40 minutes. (If the oven is any hotter than that, the heat will reach the eggs too quickly and the custard will become grainy.) Check after 25 minutes. Test for doneness by jiggling the custard. The center should be just set, not too firm.

Remove the pan from the oven. Then remove the dish from the hot water. Allow to cool.

If you are using individual ramekins, run a thin knife around the edge and invert on a plate. If it is in a large dish, spoon the custard out onto serving plates.

Yield: Four servings

Food Processor Ice Creams

To insure success it is crucial that a powerful food processor like a Robot Coupe™ or Cuisinart™ be used.

Ingredients for Vanilla Ice Cream
- 1/3 cup granulated sugar
- 2 cups heavy cream
- 1 cup half-and-half
- 1/4 teaspoon vanilla extract
- 1 small pinch kosher salt
- 1 1/2 tablespoons Bailey's Irish Cream

Method

Stir sugar, cream, half-and-half, vanilla, and salt together. Pour into ice cube trays without the divider section. Freeze hard.

Place the frozen mixture in the bowl of a food processor with the cutting blade inserted. Add 1–1 1/2 tablespoons Bailey's Irish Cream and purée. The consistency should be that of a fine soft ice cream.

Yield: Four servings

Ingredients for Raspberry Ice Cream
- 1/3   cup granulated sugar
- 2   cups heavy cream
- 1   cup half-and-half
- 1/4   teaspoon vanilla extract
- 1   small pinch kosher salt
- 1/2   pint fresh raspberries
- 2   tablespoons Framboise liqueur, white or pink

Method

Stir sugar, cream, half-and-half, vanilla, and salt together.

Purée three-quarters of the raspberries in a food processor and pass through a sieve to remove the seeds. Fold the purée into the cream mixture. Pour into ice cube trays and freeze until hard.

Remove the frozen mixture from the trays and place in a food processor. Dampen with 1–2 tablespoons of Framboise, and purée. Add the remaining raspberries, turning only about 5 pulses with the processor so the raspberries are in pieces, not puréed.

(This recipe can also be made with strawberries.)

Serving suggestions: Place alternating layers of poire sorbet (see page 110) and raspberry ice cream in a crystal ice cream or sherbet dish.

Yield: Four servings

Food Processor Sorbet

The food processor, because of the power of its motor and the design of its cutting blade, is particularly well suited for creating a very fast, simple, and extremely delicious sorbet. According to Escoffier, a sorbet has a texture that is drinkable, and this preparation produces that perfect consistency.

Any leftover sorbet can be frozen, chopped up, and puréed again, with the addition of the appropriate liqueur.

In some cases, a little more liquid may be necessary for proper puréeing. If so, more liqueur or water may be used.

To insure success, it is crucial that a powerful food processor like a Robot Coupe™ or Cuisinart™ be used.

Strawberry Sorbet
    1   pint strawberries, cleaned and hulled
    3   tablespoons Framboise de Bourgogne

Method

Seal the strawberries in plastic wrap and freeze until hard.

Place the frozen strawberries in a food processor with the Framboise de Bourgogne. Purée with the cutting blade until it becomes a thick, but not runny, liquid. Spoon into sorbet glasses.

Yield: Four servings

Variations

- Poire: Peel, core, and cube 2 large Comice pears. Dip the cubes into acidulated water (see page 221), then wrap in plastic wrap and freeze until hard. When they are frozen through, put them into a food processor with 3 tablespoons Poire William, purée and spoon into sorbet glasses.

Pink Grapefruit Sorbet: Combine 1/2 cup freshly squeezed pink grapefruit juice, 1/2 cup sugar syrup (see page 222), juice of 1/4 lemon, and 1/2 teaspoon grated lime rind. Combine ingredients and pour into ice cube trays. Freeze until solid. Put the frozen cubes into a food processor and purée.

Cucumber Salad

2 cucumbers
1 1/2 teaspoons kosher salt
1/2 cup crème fraîche or sour cream
3 grinds black pepper
1 heaping teaspoon fresh dill, finely chopped, plus extra sprigs
1 1/2 tablespoons white wine vinegar
1 tablespoon red onion, roughly chopped
1 bunch watercress

Method

Peel and thinly slice the cucumbers. Place them in a noncorrosive bowl and sprinkle with 1 teaspoon of the salt. Toss well. Refrigerate for 30 minutes.

Drain the cucumbers well and toss with the crème fraîche. Add the remaining 1/2 teaspoon salt, pepper, dill, and vinegar, then toss. Stir in the red onion, and sprinkle with sprigs of dill. Serve immediately on a bed of watercress.

To assure that each taste stands out on its own, do not let the salad sit too long after tossing.

Yield: Four servings

Variations

- To make a wonderful summer soup, place ingredients, with the addition of 1/2 cup water and a pinch of salt, in a food processor and purée. Chill and serve very cold.
- Add 1/4 teaspoon ground cumin before puréeing.

Banana Mousse Pie

One 8- or 9-inch pie crust, baked (see page 212)
Apricot glaze (see page 53)
5 ripe bananas
Juice of 1 lemon
5 tablespoons soft unsalted butter
1 tablespoon, plus 1 teaspoon confectioner's sugar
3 cups heavy cream
1/4 teaspoon vanilla extract
1/4 teaspoon grated lime rind
1/4 teaspoon lime juice

Method

Purée 3 of the bananas in a food processor. Add the lemon juice. Divide the butter into 5 pieces and add, a piece at a time, to the mixture. Mix until nearly liquid. Add 1 tablespoon confectioner's sugar. Set aside at room temperature.

In a bowl over ice, beat 2 cups of the cream until medium stiff. Fold banana mixture, a third at a time, into the cream. Refrigerate.

Seal the pie crust with apricot glaze. Place a layer of thinly sliced bananas that have been dipped into acidulated water (see page 221) over the apricot glaze. Pour the banana mousse over the bananas. Arrange another layer of sliced bananas over the mousse. Chill in the refrigerator.

Before serving, top the pie with the other 1 cup of cream, whipped medium thick and flavored with vanilla, grated lime rind, lime juice, and 1 teaspoon confectioner's sugar. This can be put into a pastry tube and piped on, or it can be mounded over the pie.

Variation

- Instead of sealing with apricot glaze, brush melted chocolate over the interior of the pie crust.

Carpaccio

1   pound filet of beef, completely trimmed of fat and gristle

Wrap the beef in aluminum foil and place it in the freezer long enough to firm only. This will make it easier to slice thin. Do not freeze! Freezing will make the water expand and break the tissues of the meat, destroying the texture.

Remove the meat from the freezer. Unwrap it, and cut across the grain in very thin slices. Place the slices between sheets of waxed paper large enough for the meat to spread. Using a meat stamp or a meat mallet, pound gently until the slices become large and paper-thin, taking care not to break them. You should be able to see light through the slices.

1/4–1/2 teaspoon fine olive oil
1 teaspoon red wine vinegar or sherry wine vinegar
1 leek, white part only, cleaned and chopped
1/8 cup finely grated or shaved grana
24–28 capers
Black pepper, coarsely ground

Method

Arrange 2–3 slices on each plate. Drizzle the olive oil and vinegar very lightly over the meat. Sprinkle with the leek and grana and grind black pepper over. Place a few capers to the side.

Yield: Four servings

Variations

Non-traditional, but very tasty, sauces can be used in place of the oil and vinegar:

- Top the slices with 1 cup mayonnaise (see page 208), blended with
  2 anchovies, mashed with a fork,
  1 tablespoon garlic purée, or 2 cloves freshly chopped garlic,
  1/2 shallot, finely chopped,
  1 tablespoon capers,
  1 tablespoon cornichons, chopped,
  1 large pinch cayenne pepper,
  1/4 teaspoon grainy mustard,
  6 grinds black pepper.
- Top the slices with 1 cup mayonnaise mixed with 1 1/2 tablespoons grainy mustard.
- Top the slices with 1 cup mayonnaise mixed with 1 tablespoon finely chopped shallot, 2 teaspoons finely chopped jalapeño peppers, 1/2 teaspoon juice from the jalapeño jar, 5 grinds black pepper, and 1 1/2 teaspoons fresh lemon juice

Salmon Mousseline

Understanding the natural albumin content of the meat or fish to be used in a mousseline is crucial to understanding how to produce the dish. It is the albumin that is responsible for taking in the cream, which contains trapped air bubbles that give it lightness—and lightness is the key to the texture of this recipe. For instance, scallops naturally have enough albumin to obviate the addition of egg whites. Other meats and fish may require egg whites to increase the albumin content of the purée.

If this recipe is followed and watched carefully, the resulting mousseline will be incomparable in texture. Many modern-day recipes omit some of the important steps necessary to achieve this result. They simplify, and thereby only approximate what the dish should be, but do not fully achieve its wonder—therein lies the difference. In cooking, many times, two percent is the difference between a very good preparation and an excellent one. For a mousseline, that two percent *is all!*

The cream in a mousseline works in two ways: first as a binding agent, second as a lifting agent. It's important to pay attention to the word *lifting*, as opposed to thinking in terms of rising. A balloon-type whisk will incorporate more air into a mixture than a rotary-type beater or a processor will. When heat hits the air it expands and *pushes* up. Therefore, the more air, the bigger the push. It doesn't gently rise upward—it pushes upward.

Ingredients for Mousseline

- 1 pound cleaned fresh salmon, completely boned, skinned, and roughly chopped
- 1/2 egg white
- 1 1/2 teaspoons kosher salt
- 1 large pinch white pepper
- 1 tiny pinch nutmeg, freshly ground
- 2 cups heavy cream, chilled

Ingredients for the center of the Mousseline

- 3–4 medium shrimp (16's), peeled, deveined, and cut into 1-inch pieces
- 1 fresh tomato, peeled, seeded, and chopped, or 2 canned tomatoes. Take special care to remove all seeds.
- 1 pinch kosher salt
- 2 grinds black pepper
- 1 tablespoon flat parsley leaves, roughly chopped

Method

Purée the fish in a food processor. Then add the egg white, salt, white pepper, and nutmeg. Process for 1 minute. Make sure that all the egg white is completely blended into the fish.

Put the purée in a chilled bowl, then place it in an ice-filled bowl. This will keep the preparation cold as you add the cream. If you use a mixer, use one that has a whisk-type beater, or whisk by hand. At medium speed, begin to beat the puréed ingredients. Slowly add 1 1/2 cups of the cream in a thin stream. Watch to make sure that the purée is taking in all of the cream.

In a separate bowl, beat the remaining 1/2 cup heavy cream until the beater begins to make traces on the surface. It should be a soft whipped cream, not stiff.

With a folding motion, fold the whipped cream into the fish mixture, taking care not to deflate it.

Mix the shrimp, tomato, salt, black pepper, and parsley. Set aside.

Lightly butter a loaf pan or terrine. Spread half of the mousseline into the pan. Gently even out the surface with a spatula, and move some of the mixture up the sides of the pan. Spoon the shrimp mixture in a narrow line down the middle. Add the rest of the mousseline, completely encasing the shrimp, and smooth the top.

Cover the pan with aluminum foil, leaving space at the top for expansion, and seal the edges tightly. Place the pan in another larger pan and add hot water to reach three-quarters of the way up the sides of the mousseline pan. Bake in a 350° F. oven for 35–40 minutes. Check occasionally to make sure that the oven temperature stays constant and that the water never boils.

When the mousseline is done, it should be slightly puffed and have a set feeling to it, springy to the touch in the center. Remove the pans from the oven and allow the mousseline to sit in the hot water for another 5 minutes. Remove the mousseline pan from the water.

If the mousseline is to be served immediately, allow it to rest for 15 minutes. Then place a plate over the pan and quickly invert. It should unmold easily. A residue of liquid exudes from the mold when it is turned out; take care not to spill the hot juices on your hands.

Slice the mousseline into 3/4-inch slices and place on warm plates. The mousseline can be sauced with a beurre blanc (see page 209) or a delicately seasoned hollandaise (see page 207).

If the mousseline is not to be served right away, it can be cooled completely, covered and stored in the refrigerator for one day. Unmold before serving and cut into 3/4-inch slices. Place the slices on a baking sheet and cover tightly with aluminum foil. Place in a 350° F. oven for 8–10 minutes. It should repuff slightly and be completely hot through. *Careful!* If the mousseline slices are heated for too long, they will collapse.

Yield: Four servings

Variations

- Substitute filet of sole for the salmon, and add 2 tablespoons chopped parsley to the purée. In the center use 5–6 roughly chopped sea scallops, and substitute 1/2 teaspoon tarragon leaves for the parsley.
- Substitute scallops for the salmon and omit the egg white. In the center use chopped scallops or lobster meat mixed with fresh basil leaves or chives.

Quenelles

Prepare mousseline recipe (see page 115), omitting ingredients for the center.

    1   tablespoon kosher salt

Method

Fill a deep pot with 3–4 inches of water and bring it to just below a simmer. Stir in the salt.

Take a heaping spoonful of mousseline, and, using another spoon, round it out to form a smooth egglike shape. Ease the spoonful into the hot water. The quenelle will leave the spoon and float in the water. Repeat the process, but do not crowd the pan. The water should be deep enough for all the quenelles to float without touching the bottom.

Poach each quenelle for 4–5 minutes on the first side. Turn over very gently with a slotted spoon, and poach an additional 3–4 minutes. Remove the quenelles with a slotted spoon and drain well.

Place on heated plates and sauce with a beurre blanc (see page 209) or hollandaise sauce (see page 207).

Yield: Four servings

Chapter VII

Chaud-Froid Brioches with Spun Sugar

Heat

...and its application

Heat is a technical term used for many types of cooking processes. Heat is a crucial element, and its proper application is essential to the preparation of food. In its true nature, it causes chemical reactions. It actively changes the molecular structure of the elements. For instance, heating egg yolks to a certain temperature expands the molecules, permitting them to accept more of the oily elements in a sauce. Keeping a stock below the boiling point permits the albumin in the meat to be released, rise, and be removed. The higher heat of boiling locks in the albumin, homogenizing it into the liquid, making the stock cloudy.

Heat is magic. It takes one element, or many, and completely changes their nature. One of the simplest and most interesting preparations that demonstrates the effect of heat is a basic cream sauce. Cream sauces do not need a thickening agent... heat is their thickening agent. When the temperature is brought high enough to evaporate the water in the cream, it naturally thickens.

When used to reduce a sauce, heat concentrates the essence of the taste that is desired by removing the extraneous liquid.

Heat may take many forms. In the preparation of a steak, it may first be used to sear the outside of the meat, closing the capillaries and enclosing the juices. It does not just give it color. The temperature is then lowered to produce the desired degree of doneness throughout. When the meat is taken off of the heat to rest, the capillaries open up again, so that the juices can run back to the outer edges of the meat.

Heat takes many forms, whether it be poaching, where there is never any boiling, low simmering, a high boil, or the use of steam to just slightly wilt an ingredient. There are times, as in a beurre blanc, when the addition of ice-cold butter to a hot liquid brings down the heat of the pan, which is necessary to keep the butter from breaking.

Heat is not only applied over a burner or in an oven. The heat of the ingredients, whether they be eggs or meat brought to room temperature, or ice-cold butter used in a pastry dough, is crucial to the success of a preparation. These essentials are often the difference between a perfectly made and easy-to-handle pie crust and one that is an absolute nightmare for the cook. Too much heat or too slow a heat can ruin the texture and flavor of meat, oil, garlic, or almost any substance. It can bring out the bitterness in garlic if it is browned too much, or the mildness of garlic when it is gently roasted. The right temperature of the oil for cooking a beignet makes the difference between its seizing and holding together—making it possible for the taste of each element to exude throughout the beignet while remaining moist inside and golden brown on the outside—and its turning black on the outside while remaining raw at the center.

Vegetable Curry with Hot Tortilla Chips

This vegetable dish demonstrates both the hot of the curry spice and the heat used in the preparation.

The heat from the curry, cayenne pepper, and the cooking process is counterbalanced by the coldness of the cucumbers that are stirred in at the last moment. These blend with the crispness of the tortillas.

Ingredients for the Tortillas
- 6 fresh soft tortillas (or fresh frozen)
- 1/2 cup clear oil, soy or corn
- 1/4 teaspoon cumin seed, freshly ground
- 1 teaspoon kosher salt

Ingredients for the Curry
- 1 cup water
- 1/2 onion, finely diced
- 1/2 cup carrot, finely diced
- 1/4 cup sweet red pepper, finely diced
- 1/4 cup celery, finely diced
- 3/4 cup zucchini, finely chopped
- 1/2 cup yellow summer squash, finely chopped
- 1/2 cup chicken stock (see page 204)
- 1 teaspoon curry powder, or to taste
- 1 1/2 teaspoons kosher salt
- 1 pinch cayenne pepper
- 1/2 tablespoon garlic purée or 1 clove garlic, finely chopped
- 1/4 cup good-quality chutney, such as Major Grey's
- 3/4 cup cucumbers, peeled, seeded, and diced well and chilled

Method for Tortilla Chips

Cut each tortilla into eight pieces. Heat the oil in a heavy-bottomed skillet until almost smoking. Reduce heat to medium-low and add the tortilla chips in small batches. Do not crowd the pan; they will not brown evenly if too crowded. Since they cook very quickly, small batches are easier to handle. Cook until lightly brown, about 2 minutes. Remove the chips from the pan and drain on paper towels. When they are all done, place the chips in a bowl and sprinkle with ground cumin and salt. Set aside.

Method for Curry

Put water and onion in a medium-size saucepan. Gently simmer, covered, for about 8–10 minutes.

Add the carrots, cover, and simmer for 2–3 minutes.

Add the red pepper and celery. Cook, covered, for about 5 minutes.

Add the zucchini and yellow squash and cook, covered, for about 5 minutes.

Add the stock, curry, salt, cayenne, and garlic. Cook, uncovered, at a high simmer for 15–20 minutes, until the mixture reduces and thickens. It should have the consistency of porridge.

Remove from the heat and allow to cool for 15 minutes. Stir in the chutney and cold pieces of cucumber. Taste for seasoning.

Serve in a bowl on a large plate, surrounded with tortilla chips.

Yield: Four servings

Standing Rib Roast

The high heat method utilizes a short injection of high heat and then depends upon the more gentle effect of the residual heat. It also shows the degree to which meat will continue to cook after the source of heat has been removed.

Standing rib roast of beef
Garlic purée, or garlic cloves, sliced
Kosher salt
Black pepper, freshly ground

Rub the ribs all over with garlic purée or with cut cloves of garlic. Season with salt and pepper.

Place the roast on a rack in a roasting pan and cook in a preheated 500° F. oven for 5 minutes per pound. *Do not open* the oven! After the cooking time has passed, turn off the oven and leave the door closed for a total of 2 hours, including cooking time.

Note: If the roast weighs 12 pounds or more, cut it into equal portions and proceed with the recipe, cooking both halves at the same time.

Have the butcher give you the exact weight of the piece, and be sure to remember it!

Baked Spinach

2 pounds spinach leaves, well washed, drained
Kosher salt
Black pepper, freshly ground
3 tablespoons fresh bread crumbs
1/4 cup olive oil

Method

Chop the spinach by cutting vertically, then horizontally.

Press the spinach into an oiled gratin dish or pie plate. Sprinkle lightly with salt, pepper, and bread crumbs. Dribble olive oil over, and bake at 450° F. for 10 minutes. Reduce to 375° F. and bake for 20 minutes longer.

Yield: Four servings

Beignets

Savory Beignets

1	cup water
2	teaspoons kosher salt
6	tablespoons unsalted butter
1	cup flour
4	eggs
1/2	teaspoon black pepper, freshly ground
	Oil for frying

Method

In a heavy-bottomed saucepan, bring the water, salt, and butter to a boil. Remove from the heat. Pour the flour all at once into the liquid. Immediately start beating with a wooden spoon until the mixture begins to hold together and leave the sides of the pan. If this does not happen in a reasonable period of time, approximately 2 minutes, return the pan to the heat for about 20–30 seconds, beating constantly. This added heat will pull it together.

Remove from heat. Break in one egg at a time and beat until the mixture comes together in a ball. Repeat until all the eggs are used. The dough should adhere to the spoon but have some yield. If it is too stiff, beat in another egg yolk. Add pepper and stir it through.

Let the dough cool. It can be refrigerated for one day, but let it reach room temperature before cooking.

After the dough has been flavored (see below), heat 4 inches of a clear oil, like soy or corn oil in a large pot. Test with a deep-fat thermometer; the temperature should be 360° F.

Holding the spoon close to the oil to minimize splatter, carefully push full tablespoons of batter off the spoon with the index finger of your opposite hand. Make sure that you avoid any hot oil splatter. Do not crowd the pan. Cook the beignets for 3–4 minutes. They have a tendency to turn themselves over during the cooking process because of changes in density. If this does not happen, turn them with a slotted spoon when they become golden brown. Remove to a baking pan lined with paper towels. Place in a warm oven until they are all cooked.

Serve approximately three beignets per person as an appetizer. Since the beignets have a tendency to roll around, they can be anchored to the plate by dipping them in a sauce, or by putting a small pool of sauce on the plate and anchoring the beignets to it.

Beignets can be flavored in any number of ways:

- Add chopped herbs.
- Marinate 3/4 cup chopped sea scallops or bay scallops in 1 tablespoon soy sauce for 20 minutes. Add this to the mixture along with 1 tablespoon chopped chives. Serve beignets with crème fraîche; or with soy sauce diluted with a little water, sprinkled with chopped chives, chopped ginger, and minced garlic.
- Add 1/2 cup grated grana, 1/2 cup 1/2-inch cubes of mozzarella, and 1/2 cup prosciutto. Serve beignets with cold or hot tomato sauce or with pesto sauce.
- Marinate 3/4 cup cubed raw shrimp in 1 tablespoon soy sauce for 20 minutes. Add to the dough. Serve beignets with crème fraîche, sour cream, or soy diluted with water, freshly grated ginger, and chopped scallion tops.
- Add 1/2 cup chopped smoked salmon, and 1 tablespoon chopped chives or dill.
- Add 3/4 cup chopped double-smoked bacon and 2 jalapeños, chopped. Serve beignets with salsa (see page 205).
- Add 3/4 cup cubed pâté de campagne and 1/4 cup finely chopped leeks, white part only. Serve with rémoulade sauce (see page 205).

Sweet Beignets

Follow the recipe for Savory Beignets, but omit the salt and pepper, and add 1 tablespoon sugar, 1/2 teaspoon cinnamon, and 1/8 teaspoon ground ginger.

Optional: Add 1/8 teaspoon of ground nutmeg or 5 raspings of fresh nutmeg.

Serve beignets sprinkled with powdered sugar and crème fraîche, or topped with your favorite jam, thinned with a little liqueur.

Variation

- Add 1/2 cup currants soaked in Mandarin Napoleon Brandy; or 1/2 cup skinned, chopped peaches or plums, or sour pitted cherries, or pears.

Cream Puffs

On a greased cookie sheet put 1 tablespoon of sweet batter for each cream puff, keeping them 2 inches apart. Bake in a 450° F. oven for 5 minutes. Reduce the heat to 375° F., and cook 20 minutes longer. Remove from the oven and lower the temperature to 200° F.

Make a small slit in the side of each puff with a sharp knife. Return the puffs to the oven for another 15 to 20 minutes to dry out the moist interior.

Remove, and allow to cool.

Cut off the tops of the puffs. If there is any moist interior remaining, remove this wet part with the tines of a fork, and dry out for another 30 minutes, then fill.

Some fillings might be:

- Flavored heavy cream, using a liqueur or an extract.
- Chopped bits of fruit and crème fraîche.
- Chocolate or fruit mousse, possibly incorporated with bits of fresh fruit.
- Whipped cream and purée of raspberries folded with chopped strawberries.

Filled sweet cream puffs can also be served with chocolate or fresh fruit sauce spooned over the top.

To make a savory cream puff, follow the instructions above, using the savory batter.

Some savory fillings might be:

- Curried tuna fish salad.
- Chicken in a cream sauce.
- Fish in a cream sauce.

Shrimp and Scallops on Linguine (High Heat Method)

The success of this recipe depends upon the ability to handle the steps properly. The technique is to take the heat off the bottom of the pan with the wine as quickly as possible, so that when the butter is added it does not break but becomes a beurre blanc sauce.

1/4	cup oil, half fine olive oil and half soy oil
12	shrimp, cleaned and deveined, tail shells left on
2	teaspoons garlic purée or 1 teaspoon minced fresh garlic
1	tablespoon shallot, finely chopped
1/2	cup dry white wine
1/2	pound bay scallops
3/4	cup unsalted butter, cut into 8 pieces
1	teaspoon kosher salt, or more

Freshly ground black pepper to taste
Parsley, finely chopped
1 pound linguine, cooked al dente

Both the shrimp and scallops are rinsed and dried so as not to lower the heat with residual water when placed in the skillet.

Method

Put the oil in a skillet and heat until almost smoking. Add the shrimp and stir for about 30 seconds to pink them. Push the shrimp to one side and add the garlic and shallots. Make sure that they have contact with the pan. Stir for about 20 seconds, then toss with the shrimp. Add the white wine and toss. Add the scallops, and continue to cook until some of the wine evaporates, approximately 20 seconds.

Add two pieces of butter and stir constantly. As the contents continue to heat and bubble, add each consecutive piece of butter and stir quickly until 7 pieces of butter have been combined into the sauce.

Remove from the heat and check for salt before the addition of the last piece of butter. Add salt and pepper to taste.

Sprinkle with parsley.

Serve over small mounds of linguine, and with lots of bread, because the sauce has a "dunkessence" that is exquisite.

Yield: Four servings

Stuffed Leg of Lamb

This high-heat method ensures tenderness and cooks the lamb to a perfect medium-rare.

One 6–7-pound leg of lamb
3 tablespoons olive oil
2 cloves garlic, finely chopped
1 medium onion, coarsely chopped
1/4 pound prosciutto, roughly chopped
1/2 cup pitted Ligurian or Italian black olives
1 large pinch kosher salt
5 sprigs fresh thyme, leaves only
2 pounds fresh spinach, well washed, heavy stems removed
1 egg yolk
1/2 teaspoon black pepper, freshly ground

Method

Have the butcher bone without splitting and ask him to remove the "fell." Weigh before stuffing.

Put 2 tablespoons of olive oil in a skillet and gently cook the garlic and onion for about 10 minutes, or until they are translucent. Add the prosciutto, cover, and cook over medium-low heat for about 5 minutes. Stir in the olives, salt, and thyme.

In another skillet, put the remaining 1 tablespoon olive oil and heat over high heat. Toss in the spinach, with the water that is clinging to it. Cover, and cook for about 2 minutes, or until the spinach is wilted. Remove from the heat and allow to cool.

With your fingers squeeze the spinach to remove any excess moisture. Put the spinach and the onion mixture in a food processor and add the egg yolk. Rough-chop and mix well.

Push the mixture into the cavity of the lamb. Tie both ends and two or three times around the middle. Brush with some extra olive oil and sprinkle with black pepper and salt.

Cook 5 minutes per pound at 500° F. in a preheated oven. At the end of the cooking time, turn off the oven, but *do not open* the oven until the lamb has been in for a total of 2 hours.

Serve this lamb cold with a grainy mustard on the side.

Yield: Four servings

Potato Salad with Jalapeños and Sweet Red Peppers

This potato salad should always be served on cold, crisp greens to serve as a contrast to the heat of the jalapeños. (Note: The jalapeño pepper is extremely hot, therefore your own discretion is called upon.)

- 1 1/2 pounds tiny new potatoes, halved
- 3 tablespoons good vinegar
- 1/4 cup dry white wine
- 1/4 cup olive oil
- 1 tablespoon finely chopped jalapeño peppers, or to taste
- 1 1/2 tablespoons shallots, finely diced
- 1/2 sweet red pepper, skinned, and medium diced
- Kosher salt to taste

Method

Bring 3 quarts of salted water to a rapid boil and add the potatoes. Cook for approximately 15 minutes, until fork-tender. Make sure they do not become too soft. Remove from the heat and drain, but do not cool.

Put the hot potato halves in a bowl. Add the vinegar and wine and toss well. Add the olive oil and toss again. Gently stir in the jalapeños, sweet red pepper, and shallots. Add salt to taste.

Yield: Four servings

Turnips en Papillote

Hermetically sealing the turnips in this way permits them to steam in their own vapor.

- 4 medium-size white turnips, peeled at least 1/4-inch into the flesh to remove the bitter outer skin
- 1 1/2 tablespoons unsalted butter
- 1 large pinch kosher salt

Method

Place the peeled turnips on a large piece of heavy-duty aluminum foil. Add the butter and salt. Completely seal them in the foil, making sure that there are no holes. Place on a cookie sheet in a 350° F. oven for 35 minutes, or until turnips are soft all the way through. Check by opening the foil and piercing with a thin-bladed instrument. If they are not done, reseal and continue to cook for a few more minutes. They cook quickly toward the end, so check often.

Remove the turnips from the oven and allow to rest for 1–2 minutes. Open the foil carefully. They can be served whole or sliced.

Yield: Four servings

Tarte Tatin

Sugar taken to its highest heat in a tart Tatin. You will note that it moves from a soft ball to a hard ball stage, then hard crack before becoming caramel. If it is not removed immediately the sugar will rapidly burn and carbonize.

Ingredients for Crust
- 1 cup unbleached flour
- 1 tablespoon granulated sugar
- 1 pinch kosher salt
- 5 tablespoons cold unsalted butter
- 2 tablespoons chilled vegetable shortening or lard
- 1/4 cup cold water

Ingredients for Tarte
- 2 tablespoons soft unsalted butter
- 1/2 cup granulated sugar
- 2 tablespoons water
- 1 teaspoon white wine vinegar
- 4–6 pears, peeled, quartered, cored, and dipped into acidulated water

Method

Sift the flour, sugar, and salt together. Cut butter and shortening into the dry ingredients with a food processor or by hand with a pastry cutter. Add the water and mix until it forms a ball. This should be done as quickly as possible, with little handling. Wrap the dough in plastic wrap and chill for at least 2 hours.

Spread the soft butter in an 8- or 9-inch heavy-bottomed metal-handled skillet. Add the sugar, water, and vinegar. Place over medium heat. Cook and swirl until it becomes liquid and the sugar is completely dissolved. Continue to cook until the mixture begins to color, or caramelize. When the sugar begins to brown, it goes very quickly, so do not leave the pan or let it get too brown, as it will continue to cook for a few minutes from its residual heat.

Remove the skillet from the heat and allow to cool for 4–5 minutes. Arrange the quartered pears in a circle in the skillet with the peeled side of the pears down and the pointed end toward the center. Roll out the crust to a 3/8-inch thickness. Center the crust over the pears, pushing the edges down and in against the edge of the pan with the back of a spoon. Pierce 5–6 holes in the crust. Cook in a 425° F. oven for 10 minutes. Lower the temperature to 375° F. and bake for another 15–20 minutes, until the crust is golden and crispy.

Remove the skillet from the oven and place it on top of the stove over a low heat. Sharply jerk the handle from side to side; this releases the fruit from the bottom. Remove from the heat and place a large plate over the skillet. Using two potholders, and being careful of the hot juices, quickly invert. Slowly lift the skillet from the tart. If any of the pieces of fruit stick to the bottom, gently remove them with a spatula and place them back on the tart.

The tart should sit for 10 minutes before serving, because it is very hot at this point. It also can be served cool, or you can reheat it. It is best accompanied with lightly whipped cream.

Yield: Six servings

Egg-Roll Satchels

Ingredients for the Egg-Roll Wrappers
- 1   cup unbleached flour
- 1/4   teaspoon kosher salt
- 1   egg
- 1   cup water
- 2   leeks, green part only, cut into strips 1/4-inch wide and 4 inches long
- Oil for frying

Method

Place the flour, salt, and egg in a food processor. Process with the cutting blade. Add the water and continue to mix. Pour the batter, which should be the consistency of heavy cream, through a fine sieve to make sure that all lumps are removed. Let the batter rest for 20 minutes.

Prepare a crêpe pan by balling up waxed paper, dipping it into a light oil, and swirling it around all sides of the pan, so that the pan is lightly filmed. Place the pan over medium heat. Check the temperature of the pan by putting a drop of water in the center. If it dances and evaporates immediately, the pan is hot enough.

Pour 1 tablespoon batter into the pan, tilting and swirling it. Pour off any excess into the batter bowl. Place back on the heat. Cook until the egg-roll wrapper starts to pull away from the sides of the pan, about 1 minute. Peel it off and put it on a plate. Repeat this step until all the wrappers have been made. Cover them with a damp cloth as you stack them, to prevent their drying out.

Put the filling of your choice (see below) into the center of each egg-roll wrapper. Pull the sides of the wrapper up around the filling, to form a small satchel.

Use a ribbon of leek to tie and close each egg-roll satchel. Make sure that the ribbon is long enough to knot.

In a deep pan, heat 2 1/2–3 inches of light oil to 360° F. Test with a thermometer, or put a small piece of bread into the oil; if it turns golden brown in about 1 minute, the oil is ready to use. Put the satchels into the oil. Do not crowd the pan. Fry for about 1 1/2 minutes, until they are golden brown and crisp. Drain on paper towels and place in a warm oven until they are all cooked.

Yield: Approximately 24 egg-roll wrappers.

Fillings

- A cube of mozzarella with chopped sun-dried tomatoes and cracked black pepper.
- Leftover minced chicken, beef, or lamb, with chopped shallots and black pepper.

- Sausage, removed from its casing and rolled into tiny balls, with a herb of your choice.
- A finely chopped vegetable mixture, such as cabbage, onions, and carrots, lightly cooked in butter.
- Raw shellfish, such as shrimp or scallops, chopped with shallots and onions.
- Cold balls of chili, with a dot of cheddar and chopped onion.

Serve filled egg-rolls with a dipping sauce such as:

- Soy sauce, with chopped garlic and scallions.
- Salsa (see page 205).
- Light tomato sauce, hot or cold (see page 210).
- Aioli (see page 208).

Haricots Verts with Bay Scallops and Sherry Wine Vinegar

3/4 pound haricots verts or very young fresh thin string beans
1 tablespoon soy oil
4 tablespoons unsalted butter
3/4 pound bay scallops
2 tablespoons fine sherry wine vinegar mixed with 2 tablespoons water
1 1/2 large pinches kosher salt
6 grinds black pepper
2 tablespoons pignoli nuts, lightly browned in a 350° F. oven

Method

Nip the ends and remove the strings of the haricots verts. Wash, and cook them in boiling salted water until they are al dente, checking often after 3 minutes. Cool rapidly in cold water. Drain well. Arrange nests of beans on 4 plates, and refrigerate.

Heat the oil and 1 tablespoon of butter in a stainless steel skillet. When it is hot, add the scallops. Sauté over high heat, moving them very rapidly, for approximately 1 1/2 minutes, or until they are lightly browned.

Add the sherry vinegar. Cook for another 30 seconds. Add salt and pepper and stir in the remaining 3 tablespoons butter until melted.

Spoon the scallops over the nests which will catch and hold them, then drizzle on the sauce. Sprinkle the pignoli nuts on top and serve.

Yield: Four servings

Pan-Broiled Swordfish with a Lemon-Basil Vinaigrette

This recipe uses a radiant-heat cooking process and requires a pan that has ridges on the bottom. These special pans create the radiant heat effect. The flesh of the fish does not sit in the juice or fat, but is raised by the ridges and is self-basted by its juices splattering back on the flesh.

- 2 tablespoons fine red wine vinegar or Italian balsamic vinegar
- 1/3 cup olive oil
- Kosher salt to taste
- 1/4 teaspoon black pepper, freshly ground
- 2 lemons, peeled and sliced into very thin rounds
- 1/4 cup fresh basil chiffonade
- Four 3/4-inch-thick swordfish steaks, about 6–7 ounces each, marinated in fine olive oil for 15 minutes

Method

Place the vinegar in a small bowl. Slowly whisk in olive oil. Add salt, pepper, sliced lemons, and basil. Stir until combined. Set aside.

Heat the pan until quite hot. Place the filets on the ridges. Cook over medium heat for 3 minutes. Turn the filets 90 degrees. Cook for 3 more minutes to create cross-hatch grid marks. Turn the fish over and cook about 4 more minutes, or until it is cooked through. Test with a sharp knife or fork. The flesh should yield easily.

When the steaks are cooked, place them on hot plates. Stir the sauce well to reamalgamate it. Spoon over the fish filets. Pass the peppermill.

Yield: Four servings

Chaud-Froid Brioches

This elegant dessert employs meringue to insulate the cold fruit salad from the heat necessary to brown the meringue.

    4   fresh brioches, at room temperature (These should be the classic form of brioche with knobs on top)
    3/4 cup fresh fruit salad, well chilled
    1/4 cup sliced almonds
    Meringue (see page 219)

Method

With a small sharp knife, cut a well in each brioche, leaving a 1/2-inch wall all around. Fill the wells with fruit salad and some of its juices. Replace top.

Use a spatula to completely encase the brioches with 1/2 inch of uncooked meringue. Cover the tops with meringue, ending with a decorative swirl. Sprinkle lightly with sliced almonds. Place the brioches on a baking sheet and bake at 425° F. for 4–5 minutes. Check after 2–3 minutes to make sure that they are not taking color too fast. Serve warm. They can be eaten after they cool, but the warm-cold effect will be lost.

Yield: Four servings

Steak Putanesca

4   grinds black pepper
4   well-trimmed rib eye steaks, about 1" thick
2   tablespoons shallot, chopped
2   teaspoons garlic purée or 1 clove garlic, finely chopped
2   whole Italian canned tomatoes, chopped (reserve the liquid)
1   tablespoon sun-dried tomato, chopped
1/8   cup Ligurian olives, pitted and chopped
1/2   teaspoon capers
1/4   teaspoon rosemary leaves
1   teaspoon red pepper flakes or chopped jalapeño
Optional: 1/4 cup glace de viande (see page 204)
1   pinch kosher salt
1   tablespoon unsalted butter
Coarsely grated grana
Fresh parsley, chopped

Method

With the heel of your hand, push freshly cracked black pepper into the steaks.

Place the steaks in a hot skillet which has been filmed with olive oil. Cook for about 3 1/2–4 minutes on each side over medium heat for rare. Do not be afraid to let the meat get brown on the outside. Remove the steaks from the pan. Place them in such a way that air can circulate under the meat to prevent steaming.

Remove all but 1 tablespoon fat from the pan. If it has burned, discard it and add butter.

Sauté shallots in the fat for 2 minutes. Add garlic purée and about 1/2 cup of the liquid from the can of tomatoes. Stir in the sun-dried tomatoes, olives, capers, rosemary, and red pepper flakes. Add the tomatoes and cook for 4 minutes. Stir in the glace de viande. Add salt. Cook for approximately 8 minutes, until sauce is slightly thickened.

Remove from the heat and allow it to stop bubbling. Stir in the juices that have drained from the steak. Then monter au beurre. Taste for seasoning. Spoon sauce over the steaks, and sprinkle with grana and parsley.

(If the steaks have gotten cold, warm them quickly in a 400° F. oven for 2–3 minutes.)

Yield: Four servings

Chapter VIII

Soft-Shell Crabs in Beurre Blanc with Swirls of Caviar

Composition

...color, balance, form

"God creates—Man assembles" was an oft-quoted Balanchine adage. This remark is just as appropriate when thinking in terms of the overall composition of a plate of food. A large part of composition is the process of elimination. In today's environment, with infinite ingredients to choose from, it becomes more and more difficult because the process of elimination has become so vast. As possibilities have been expanded, the choices, the balances, and the decisions are infinitely more complex.

Until recently, chefs permitted their creations to be served at the table by a captain or a maître. Now they have become more involved in the presentation of their dishes, not wanting to leave the actual "plating" to chance. I have found that there are times when it is "happening," and every single haricot vert falls onto the plate just perfectly, with but one twist of my wrist. There are other times when it takes a great deal of work. As in Zen, when one concentrates on the action itself, as opposed to being one with the action, it does not happen properly. I'm not suggesting that you need become a Zen master in order to plate effectively. What I am suggesting is that the mystique and overcomplication be edited out. Let the natural color and shapes of each of the dishes be permitted to speak for themselves.

I do not believe in "garnishing" a plate. The elements should give sense and movement, each taste intentionally included as an integral part of the whole, not as a decorative element.

After deciding which element should be the focal point, I work with color, texture, and shape. I generally begin by placing the most important element of the dish on the plate, then let each additional element suggest itself. Design components I frequently use are off-center masses, swirls, and height. I try to effect naturalness, as opposed to contrivance, which gives life and excitement. On a plate, height to me implies life, flatness implies death. A sauce should be shining in color, to catch and reflect light.

In recent years, fortunately, there has been a trend toward clarity in sauces. They don't mask the elements that are being sauced . . . they illuminate them. If there is a particularly beautiful element of a dish, I will often sauce the plate first, then put the element, completely exposed, on top of the sauce. For a dessert, I often use pools of crème fraîche under the subject rather than drizzling it over the top.

As in the definition of fine art, "less is more." I don't believe that the composition should ever become mere decoration. The color, balance, and form should enhance, not overwhelm, the dish.

Food in and of itself creates joy, pleasure, and magic when presented well. A pork roast beautifully rolled with cranberries and spinach in the center gives a color and taste that have a reason for being there. The elements complement the tastes, they do not just make the dish "pretty."

Crown of Shrimp

16 shrimp (8–9 shrimp to the pound, or approximately 2 ounces each)
2 tablespoons unsalted butter, clarified
Wild rice (see page 215)
Spinach (see page 214)
Beurre Blanc (see page 209)

Forty-five minutes before you plan to serve the shrimp, prepare the wild rice. Cover, and keep warm.

Twenty minutes before serving, prepare the beurre blanc. Keep warm.

Method

Holding the shrimp with the shell still on, place a shrimp on its back with its tail away from you. Insert the point of a sharp knife about 1/2 inch in from where the tail meets the body. With a gentle sawing motion, cut through the shell and the flesh along the entire length of the body. Cut through when you get to the bottom shell of the body, to split the shrimp in half. The shrimp will still be joined at the tail but will splay out. Rinse, and remove the vein. Repeat with the remaining shrimp.

Set the shrimp aside while you cook the spinach. Keep the cooked spinach warm and proceed with the shrimp.

Coat the bottom of a cookie sheet with clarified butter. Reform the shrimp into their original shape. Holding each one with the tail away from you, as in the first step, splay the bottom of the shrimp around and back on each side. The natural weight of the shrimp will cause the tail to fall forward. Place all the shrimp on the cookie sheet in this position.

Place the shrimp under a preheated, very hot broiler, about 4 inches away from the source of heat. As the shrimp cook, the tail will stand up, so it is very important to watch that the tails do not burn. The tails will brown but should not char. Cook for about 2–3 minutes, or until the tail is standing up and the shrimp is cooked through. Remove from the broiler.

Place a portion of wild rice in the center of each plate. Surround it with a ring of spinach that has been drained of excess water. Place the beurre blanc into a spouted vessel so that it can be poured in a 1-inch-wide ribbon around the spinach. Place the shrimp in the sauce, one touching the other, tails up, forming a circle.

Yield: Four servings

Fruit Soup

Other fruits can be substituted for those listed in this recipe, depending upon what is fresh in the market. However, attention must be given to the principles of balance, taste, color, and shape.

1	pint fresh raspberries or strawberries, puréed with Eau de Framboise and pressed through a sieve to remove the seeds
1	Butter Cream Cake (see page 70), prepared a day in advance and allowed to dry out slightly
1/4	cup sour cream or crème fraîche (see page 218)
1/2	recipe for Banana Mousse (see page 112)
1	peeled kiwi, cut into 1/4-inch-thick rounds, the rounds then cut in half
2	blood oranges or mandarin oranges, skin and pith removed, then sectioned
8	strawberries, split in half lengthwise
1	teaspoon currants, soaked for at least 1 hour in 2 teaspoons Chartreuse
8	sour pitted cherries, jarred or canned
12	fresh blackberries
4	teaspoons macadamia nuts, hazelnuts, or pecans, roughly chopped
8–12	fresh mint leaves

Method

Lightly cover the entire bottom of each dessert plate with raspberry purée. Place in the center a 2-inch piece of cake that has been cut into an interesting shape with a cookie cutter. Spoon the sour cream or crème fraîche over the cake, completely concealing it. Sprinkle chopped nuts over the sour cream.

Form "eggs" of banana mousse by filling a teaspoon with mousse, then gently push the mousse from the spoon onto the purée. Use one or two banana mousse eggs per person.

Divide and arrange the rest of the ingredients on the purée, taking care to balance the colors and shapes.

Lastly, add 2 or 3 mint leaves as a final compositional element.

Yield: Four servings

Filet of Sole with Beurre Blanc and Steamed Spinach

Beurre Blanc (see page 209)
4   filets of sole, 6–8 ounces each
1   teaspoon kosher salt
1/2   teaspoon black pepper, freshly ground
1   tablespoon parsley leaves, chopped
1/4   cup dry white wine
1/2   cup water
1   tablespoon shallot, chopped
1   tablespoon unsalted butter
Spinach (see page 214)

Method

Prepare the beurre blanc and keep it warm.

Lay the filets out with the skin side up. With the back of a knife, tap firmly across the filets at 1-inch intervals to prevent them from uncurling when they are rolled. Sprinkle salt, pepper, and parsley over the filets and roll from the wide end to the small end. Place them, seam side down, in a glass or stainless steel baking pan.

Pour the wine and water into the pan. Sprinkle in the shallots, and dot evenly with butter. Cover, and cook in a 400° F. oven for 6–8 minutes, until easily pierced with a thin blade.

While the fish is poaching, cook the spinach, drain it well, and keep it warm. When the fish is done, place a nest of spinach in the center of each plate. Lay the rolled filet in the nest and spoon on the beurre blanc. Grind black pepper over.

Yield: Four servings

Sour Cherry Compote

This can be served lukewarm or cold.

- 1   medium onion, thinly sliced
- 2   cloves garlic, peeled and thinly sliced
- 1/2   cup water
- 2   tablespoons sherry wine vinegar
- 1   tablespoon granulated sugar
- 1   small pinch celery seed
- 1   teaspoon green peppercorns
- 2   pinches black mustard seed
- 1   small pinch coriander seed
- 6   ounces sour pitted cherries (reserve the liquid if it is not a heavy syrup)
- 1   teaspoon arrowroot
- 1/4   cup dry white wine
- 1/4   cup blanched chopped almonds or chopped walnuts

Method

In a stainless steel saucepan, simmer the onion and garlic in the water for 6–8 minutes, until the onions have become translucent. Add the vinegar, sugar, spices, and 2 tablespoons cherry liquid. Continue to simmer for 5 minutes. Add the drained cherries.

In a small bowl, dissolve the arrowroot in the white wine.

Remove the cherry mixture from the heat. Stir in the dissolved arrowroot. Return pan to the heat and let simmer, stirring continuously, for about 2 minutes, until it thickens and turns clear. Add the nuts and stir them through.

Yield: Four servings

Braised Loin of Pork with Cranberries, Sage, and Tangerines

An interior, mosaiclike composition is created by combining ingredients with a consideration of how they will look on the cross cut.

- 2 leeks, white part only
- 1/2 cup raw whole cranberries, washed
- 1/4 cup flat parsley, finely chopped, plus 4 stems
- 1/3 teaspoon black pepper, freshly ground
- 2 pinches kosher salt
- 2 tangerines, peeled and separated
- 1/2 teaspoon tangerine rind, roughly grated
- 8 leaves fresh sage or 1/2 teaspoon dried sage
- 1 piece center-cut loin of pork about 10 inches long, boned and well trimmed
- 2 tablespoons olive oil
- 2 cups full-bodied red wine
- 8 black peppercorns
- 2 tablespoons cold unsalted butter

Method

Cut off top part of the leeks and slash horizontally to within about an inch of the base so that they will splay open for sand removal.

Put the cranberries, parsley, pepper, and salt into a food processor. Chop until coarse. Stir in 1 tangerine, the rind, and half the sage.

Cut a pocket in the pork roast; push a sharp knife all the way through the center from end to end, then cut down approximately 1/2 inch; turn the knife and cut approximately 1/2 inch in the other direction; turn the knife again and cut 1/2 inch in the third direction. This will create a triangle pattern.

Stuff the cranberry mixture into the pocket. Tie the roast in several places.

Put the roast into a hot skillet with the olive oil. Sear, fat side down first. Slowly rotate until all sides have been seared. When the roast has been thoroughly seared, place it in a casserole.

Remove the excess fat from the skillet. Deglaze the pan with wine and simmer for 3 minutes. Pour the wine over the pork roast in the casserole. Add the leeks, parsley stems, and peppercorns. Cover, and cook in a 350° F. oven for approximately 45 minutes, or until meat thermometer registers 190° F.

After 30 minutes, check the leeks to make sure they do not overcook—they should be firm but yielding. Remove them when they are tender. When done, remove the pork roast from the casserole. Place on a plate so the meat can rest. Skim the fat from the casserole and remove the cloves of garlic, if they have been added.

Strain the liquid and pour it into a skillet. Simmer to reduce the liquid until there is approximately 3/4 cup. Remove from heat.

Carve the pork into 1/2-inch-thick medallions and arrange the slices on warmed plates.

Place the skillet back on the heat, and bring to a simmer. Stir in the very cold butter, stirring rapidly to break up the butter molecules and thicken the sauce slightly. Add the rest of the sage. While the sauce is reducing, add the leeks to warm them through.

Remove the skillet from the heat, and spoon the sauce over

the medallions of pork. Arrange the leeks to one side. Place the remaining sections of tangerine, from which all of the membrane has been removed, on top of the pork.

Yield: Four servings

Variation

- Add 4 cloves garlic to the liquid in the casserole, along with the leeks, parsley stems, and peppercorns. Remove and reserve the garlic before straining the cooking liquid. Before plating, cut off the top of the garlic cloves and squeeze the essence into the center of each plate, almost as though it is butter. This will serve as a floor upon which pork medallions are placed.

Chestnut Cream with Chocolate Shavings (Monte Bianco de Maronne)

1   pound fresh chestnuts
1 1/2   cups milk
1/4   cup granulated sugar
One 2-inch piece vanilla bean
1   small pinch kosher salt
1   cup heavy cream, beaten until slightly stiff
1   ounce semi-sweet chocolate, shaved or curled

Method
   With the tip of a sharp knife, cut an X just through the skin on the flat side of each chestnut. Place them on a cookie sheet in a 350° F. oven and bake for approximately 15 minutes, or until the skin curls back. Peel away the skins, and remove the inner membrane. This should yield approximately 2 cups.

Place the chestnuts in a saucepan with milk, sugar, vanilla bean, and salt. Bring to a simmer and let simmer for about 30–40 minutes, until the milk thickens and reduces. The chestnuts should be soft. Stir occasionally to prevent sticking.

Remove the vanilla bean and allow the mixture to cool completely.

Traditionally, this mixture is puréed through a food mill to create spaghetti-like strands which are then mounded to form a peak. If you do not have a food mill, use a food processor to purée the chestnuts. While it will slightly change the appearance of the dessert, it will produce the same taste effect. Place the ingredients from the saucepan in a processor with the cutting blade. Purée. The texture will be almost like a paste when completely finished. (This can be made in advance and placed in a tightly covered container in the refrigerator for 2 or 3 days.) Before working with it again, bring it to room temperature and soften it with a wooden spoon.

Lightly spoon the purée, or squeeze through a pastry bag, into a baked pie shell or small tart shell.

Pipe the whipped cream on top, and sprinkle with chocolate curls or shavings.

Yield: Four servings

Medallions of Veal with Three Mushrooms

Medallions are 1/4-inch-thick slices; do not pound them to the thinness of scallopini.

12–16 medallions of Plume de Veau or Nature Veal, preferably from the loin, or from the leg
1/2 cup flour
2 tablespoons unsalted butter, plus 2 tablespoons cold unsalted butter
1 tablespoon olive oil
1 tablespoon shallot, finely chopped
1/3 cup dry red wine
2 ounces dried porcini, Polish, or French mushrooms, reconstituted in 1 cup water
1/2 cup liquid from the reconstituted mushrooms, finely strained
1/2 cup American champignons, quartered and sautéed in 1 tablespoon butter and 1 tablespoon oil
1/2 cup Black Forest, shiitaki, or Golden Oak mushrooms, sliced
1/2 cup glace de viande (see page 204)
1 teaspoon kosher salt
4 grinds black pepper

Method

Toss the medallions of veal in flour until they are lightly coated. Shake off all excess flour.

Heat 1 tablespoon of butter and the oil in a skillet until the butter begins to brown. Add the medallions, making sure not to crowd them. Over high heat, brown the medallions 2 minutes on each side. Remove from the skillet to a heated plate.

Pour off any excess fat from the skillet and add 1 tablespoon of the butter. Sauté the shallots for 1 1/2 minutes. Deglaze the skillet with wine. Add the reconstituted mushrooms, 1/2 cup of the mushroom liquid, finely strained, the sautéed champignons, and wild mushrooms. Cook for 3 minutes. Stir in the glace de viande. Bring to a rolling simmer, and allow to reduce for 6–7 minutes, until slightly thickened.

Add salt and pepper. Add any juices from the veal and taste for seasoning. Then monter au beurre with 2 tablespoons cold butter.

Arrange the medallions in the center of a plate and spoon the sauce and mushrooms over them.

Yield: Four servings

Soft-Shell Crabs in Beurre Blanc with Swirls of Caviar

Beurre Blanc (see page 209)
8   medium- or 12 silver-dollar-sized crabs (ask your fishmonger to clean them)
1   cup whole milk
1/2 cup flour
3   tablespoons olive oil
2   teaspoons unsalted butter
1/2 ounce fine black caviar (not lump fish caviar)

Method

Prepare the beurre blanc and keep it warm.

Rinse the crabs, and soak them in the milk for 10 minutes. Drain well, then dip them into the flour, making sure that the entire crab is covered with flour. Remove excess flour by tapping the crabs gently.

In a heavy-bottomed skillet (preferably cast iron) with a surface large enough to hold all the crabs, heat the oil and butter to a high heat. When the butter is beginning to brown, lower the heat to medium, and quickly place the crabs, top side down. Be careful when you are placing the crabs in the hot oil; they have a tendency to splatter violently. Adjust the heat so that the butter is not burning, and cook for about 2 1/2–3 minutes. Turn with a spatula, and cook for another 2 1/2–3 minutes. To test for doneness, press the crab in the center with your finger. It should be lightly springy to the touch, but it should not be soft. Remove from heat.

Put 3 tablespoons of beurre blanc on the center of each warm plate, forming a pool. Arrange the crabs around the pool, as though they were looking in. Place a small spoonful of caviar in the center of each pool, and gently swirl it through.

Yield: Four servings

Chapter IX

Pasta with Putanesca Sauce

Security Blanket

...food for the soul

For years a discussion has been going on about the difference between "masculine" and "feminine" cooking. Masculine cooking is less concerned with nutrition than presentation. Feminine cooking refers to those types of preparations that evoke sense memories. They are usually slow-cooked preparations that create a warmth and sense of well-being for all who even pass the kitchen. This food is one with the land. It includes earthy ingredients and is in no way intellectually subtle.

There is a general sense of well-being created by the aromas that are given off from the long slow cooked meats and other ingredients in this form of cooking.

It is possible to take the classics and reconsider them. By adding the ingredients at different stages you can maintain the intended textures of the ingredients. I would not cook a string bean for as long as a potato.

The tastes and feelings evoked can serve as the basis for a lovely evening, such as a dinner of polenta topped with chicken and sausage. It is a shared experience, because it requires the physical participation of all of the guests.

Chicken with Garlic, Sealed in a Crust

Ingredients for Chicken

  Two 2 1/2-pound frying chickens, cut up
  1/2 cup olive oil
  2 tablespoons kosher salt
  1 teaspoon black pepper, freshly ground
  2 whole heads of garlic, broken apart, left in their skins, with the loose filaments removed
  3–4 sprigs fresh thyme or 1/2 teaspoon dried thyme
  4 sprigs fresh oregano or 1/2 teaspoon dried oregano
  2 bay leaves
  Five 2-inch pieces of parsley stems, tied together
  4 leeks, white parts only, well washed

Ingredients for Dough

  1 1/2 cups flour
  Water as necessary, approximately 3/4 cup
  1/2 teaspoon olive oil

Method for Chicken

Place all the chicken ingredients except the bay leaves, parsley, and leeks in a casserole. Toss with your hands until everything is well lubricated. Add the bay leaves, parsley, and leeks. Cover, and set aside.

Method for Dough

Place the flour in a small bowl. Slowly add water, dribble in the oil, and mix well. The dough should be easy to handle and roll.

On a lightly floured board, roll the dough with both hands, almost like a child creating a clay snake. Stretch and roll it at the same time until it reaches a length equal to the circumference of the casserole. At this point it can be cut into smaller, more workable pieces. Use your fingers to push and pinch the dough into the crack between the casserole and its lid, to completely seal the pot.

Place the casserole in the oven and bake at 350° F. for approximately 1 hour and 20 minutes.

Remove the casserole from the oven and allow it to cool for about 5 minutes.

This dish is best when brought to the table in the sealed casserole. When the seal is broken, the garlic fragrance that rushes out can then be appreciated by everyone at the table. Remove the parsley stems, and serve.

Pass warm toasted French bread, and encourage your guests to gently squeeze the garlic from their husks onto the buttered toast.

Yield: Four servings

Cornbread Stuffing

- 3/4 cup mushrooms, sliced
- 2 tablespoons oil
- 2 tablespoons unsalted butter
- 1 large onion, roughly chopped
- Cornbread (see page 216), baked a day ahead and allowed to dry out
- 3 sage leaves
- 3 jalapeño peppers, chopped
- 1 tablespoon kosher salt
- 1 cup chicken stock (see page 204)

Method

Sauté the mushrooms in oil and 1 tablespoon butter for 5 minutes. Melt the onions in the same amount of oil and butter. Cut the cornbread into 1-inch squares. Place it in a large bowl and add the mushrooms, onions, sage, and the residual oil and fat from the pans. Add the jalapeños and stock. Toss well to soak the cornbread. Add salt.

Pack the stuffing into a baking pan and mound it slightly in the center. Dot liberally with additional butter and bake in the oven at 375° F. for 20 minutes, or until nicely browned on top.

Serve by spooning onto a plate and resting carved bird pieces on top, or place the stuffing to the side of the bird.

Yield: Four servings

Clam Soup

   1   shallot, finely chopped
1/4   red onion, finely chopped
   1   leek, white part only, finely chopped
   2   tablespoons fine olive oil
   1   carrot, coarsely chopped
2 1/2 teaspoons garlic purée, or 1 teaspoon garlic, finely chopped
   2   medium-size ripe tomatoes, peeled, seeded, and chopped
 12   fresh clams, well washed
1 1/2 cups water
1/2   cup dry white wine
   3   sprigs fresh thyme or 1/4 teaspoon dried thyme
1/2   sprig rosemary or pinch dried rosemary
   1   cup Sacramento tomato juice
   5   grinds black pepper
Kosher salt
   1   teaspoon Pernod
   1   tablespoon parsley, chopped

Method

Sauté the shallot, onion, and leek in a pan with the olive oil. Cover, and cook over low heat for about 5 minutes. Add the carrot, garlic purée, and tomatoes. Stir, then cover and cook another 10 minutes.

In a separate pan place the clams, with 1/2 cup water and white wine. Bring the liquid to a boil. Cover and cook for about 5 minutes or until the clams open. Remove the clams. Simmer the liquid until reduced by half. Strain through a fine strainer, and pour it into the vegetable mixture. Add the thyme and rosemary. Stir in the tomato juice. Add black pepper and the remaining 1 cup water. Simmer for about 10 minutes, uncovered. Salt to taste.

While this is simmering, remove the clams from the shells. Rinse them and cut them into large pieces. Drop the clams into the broth and cook for about 1 minute to warm them.

Divide the clams among the plates. Add 1/4 teaspoon Pernod to each bowl. Pour the broth over and sprinkle a large pinch of parsley on each serving.

Yield: Four servings

Corn Relish

4	cups fresh corn removed from cob or frozen corn can be substituted
1 1/2	cups white cabbage, roughly chopped
1	large onion, roughly chopped
3/4	cup sweet green peppers, roughly chopped
3/4	cup sweet red pepper, roughly chopped
1/3	cup sugar
1	tablespoon dry mustard
1 1/2	teaspoons kosher salt
1	teaspoon celery seed
1	teaspoon mustard seed
1/2	teaspoon turmeric
1 1/2	tablespoons white wine vinegar
1/2	cup water

Method

Combine all the ingredients in a stainless steel saucepan. Bring to a medium simmer and cook for about 15–20 minutes. Remove from heat and allow to cool.

This relish will keep for about a week under refrigeration.

Yield: Six to eight servings

Putanesca Sauce

- 1/2   onion, roughly chopped
- 1   tablespoon garlic purée or 2 cloves garlic, finely chopped
- 4   tablespoons olive oil
- 3   anchovy filets
- 2   sprigs fresh oregano or 1/4 teaspoon dried oregano
- 1   bay leaf
- 1/2   teaspoon red chili peppers or red pepper flakes
- 3   fresh tomatoes, peeled, seeded and chopped, or 5 canned, chopped
- 1   teaspoon kosher salt
- 1   tablespoon capers
- Black pepper, freshly ground
- 1/3   cup imported black olives, pitted
- 1/8   cup grated grana
- Optional: 1 can Italian tuna fish, well drained

Method

Melt the onion and garlic in olive oil until translucent. Stir in the anchovies until they disintegrate. Add the herbs, red pepper, tomatoes, salt, capers, pepper, and olives. Simmer gently for 20–30 minutes.

Stir in the tuna fish if you are using it.

This sauce can be served on hot pasta or on pasta cooked al dente and cooled in cold water, then served cold. Sprinkle liberally with cheese.

Yield: Four servings

Chicken Pot Pie

This old favorite is "reconsidered" and made more elegant by the addition of puff pastry, snow peas, and crème fraîche.

One 3 1/2-pound chicken, cut into pieces
Kosher salt
Black pepper, freshly ground
1/2 cup onions, sliced
1 bay leaf
3 sprigs fresh thyme or 1 teaspoon dried thyme
1 cup dry white wine
1 cup chicken stock (see page 204)
1 1/2 cups heavy cream
3/4 cup carrots, peeled and cut into thick slices or 6 tiny Belgian carrots, whole (approximately 3/4 cup)
1 stalk celery, peeled to remove strings, and cut into 1/2-inch pieces
1/2 pound small button mushrooms, trimmed and left whole. If they are larger mushrooms, trim and quarter them
1 pound puff pastry (homemade or commercially prepared)
2 egg yolks
1 tablespoon water
16 snow peas, nip the ends and remove the stem
1 tablespoon unsalted butter
Crème fraîche

Method

Lay the chicken pieces on a board and sprinkle them generously with salt and pepper.

Heat a stainless steel frying pan large enough to hold all the chicken. It is not necessary to place any oil in the pan, as the chicken will release its own fat. Brown the chicken on all sides for 8–10 minutes. Remove the chicken to a side dish.

If the fat in the pan has not burned, add the onions. However, if it has, pour off the burned fat and add 1 tablespoon unsalted butter. Cook the onions for 10–12 minutes, or until they have melted and started to turn golden.

Return the chicken to the skillet. Add the bay leaf, thyme, white wine, and stock. Reduce the heat to low, and cover the pan. Gently simmer for 15–20 minutes. Remove the pan from the heat.

Remove the chicken, and allow it to cool. When it can easily be handled, remove the meat from the bones with your fingers, and cut it into large bite-size pieces. The skin can be removed if you don't enjoy it; however, it adds a delicious flavor.

Return the pan to the heat and reduce the liquid over high heat to approximately 1 1/4 cups. Add the cream. Reduce again for 8–10 minutes, until the sauce begins to thicken. Pour the juices that have exuded from the chicken into the sauce. Taste for salt and pepper.

Divide the chicken among four ovenproof crocks. Distribute all of the vegetables, except the snow peas, among the four crocks. Ladle the sauce over the chicken.

Roll out the puff pastry to 3/16-inch thickness. Cut it into pieces large enough to cover and overhang each of the crocks by approximately 3/4 inch.

Make an egg wash by gently beating the eggs with the water. With a pastry brush, paint the top edge and 3/4 inch down the sides of the crocks with the egg wash.

Place the pieces of puff pastry over each crock as taut as possible. Then press the overhang tightly against the exterior band of the egg wash, to form a seal.

Refrigerate for at least 1 hour, or until about 30 minutes before serving.

Preheat the oven to 425° F.

Place the crocks on a baking sheet and bake for about 20–25 minutes, until the crust is well puffed and golden brown.

Serve immediately. Accompany with snow peas sautéed lightly in 1 tablespoon butter for 3–4 minutes.

Pass a bowl of crème fraîche (see page 218).

Yield: Four servings

Potatoes au-Gratin

4   Idaho potatoes
1/4   cup unsalted butter, clarified, plus 2 tablespoons unsalted butter
1/2   cup Gruyère cheese, coarsely grated
Kosher salt
Black pepper, freshly ground
1   cup heavy cream

Method

Butter an 8-by-8-by-2-inch baking dish.

Peel and thinly slice the potatoes. The slices should be about 1/8-inch thick. (Note: By slicing a thin piece from the flat side of the potato, you will have a firm surface for the potato to rest on while you are slicing it.) Rinse the slices and dry well. Layer the potatoes in the baking dish with the clarified butter, Gruyère, and salt and pepper to taste between each layer. Repeat until all the potatoes are used. On the top layer, sprinkle salt and Gruyère, but omit the pepper.

Pour the heavy cream over, then press the potatoes down slightly with your fingers. Dot with the remaining butter and cover tightly with aluminum foil. Place in a 350° F. oven and cook for 35 minutes. Remove the aluminum foil, and cook for an additional 15 minutes, to brown the top.

Yield: Four servings

Variations

- Add melted onions between the layers.
- Add garlic purée between the layers.
- Add prosciutto between the layers.

Black Bean and Madeira Soup

Rich in color, taste, and texture, with a hint of sweetness from the Madeira, this soup has a soul-warming quality.

```
1     pound black beans
1     ham bone
1/2   onion, stuck with 2 cloves
1     bay leaf
1/2   tablespoon garlic purée or 4 cloves of garlic
1/4   teaspoon cumin seed
1     celery stalk
1/2   cup onion, thinly sliced
Kosher salt
4     tablespoons dry Madeira
4     tablespoons onion, finely chopped
Sour cream
1     lime, sliced
```

Method

Cover the beans with water by 1/2 inch. Bring to a boil, then remove from the heat. Let the beans sit for 1 hour.

Add water to cover the beans by 2 inches and add the ham bone, half onion, bay leaf, garlic, cumin seed, celery, and sliced onion. Return the pot to the heat and simmer gently until the beans are soft. If the liquid evaporates too quickly, add more water or some chicken stock. The beans should always be well covered with liquid. Add salt to taste.

Remove the pot from the heat. Discard the ham bone, bay leaf, celery, and the onion with cloves.

Purée about three-quarters of the soup and add the other one-quarter of unpuréed beans to it. If the soup is too thick at this point, it can be thinned with chicken stock or water, in 1/2 cup increments, until it is like a medium porridge. Before ladling the soup into bowls, add 1 tablespoon dry Madeira to the bottom of each warmed bowl.

Top the soup with the chopped onion, a dollop of sour cream, and a wedge of lime.

Yield: Four servings

Braised Cabbage

There is a little bit of Russia and a lot of love from my grandmother in this earthy dish that combines the sweet from the slow cooking of the onions and cabbage and the sour from vinegar and green apple.

3/4 cup onions, thinly sliced
1/4 cup duck or goose fat, or olive oil
3 cups purple cabbage, thinly sliced (tightly pack measuring cup to assure the correct measurement)
2 tablespoons fine red wine vinegar or 3 tablespoons red wine
6 juniper berries
3/4 cup chicken stock (see page 204)
2 sprigs fresh thyme or 1 pinch dried thyme
1 bay leaf
Optional: Small pinch celery seed
1 green apple, cored and cubed, but not peeled

Method

Remove the core from the cabbage, most easily done by quartering it first. Slice thinly.

Simmer the onions in the fat in a covered stainless steel skillet for about 12–15 minutes. Stir in the cabbage. Cook for another 5 minutes, covered. Add the remaining ingredients, except the apple. Gently simmer, covered, for about 30 minutes.

Add the apple and cook for an additional 10 minutes, uncovered. Test to see if the cabbage is tender. Simmer longer if necessary. Add salt to taste.

The addition of red wine vinegar or red wine helps the cabbage retain its red color, as well as adding flavor.

Yield: Four servings

Maple Walnut Pie

This pie is not only delicious and completely non-sugary, but it is also an extremely simple recipe . . . one that takes virtually no time to make!

4 eggs
1/3 cup honey
2/3 cup pure maple syrup
2 tablespoons arrowroot
2 cups walnuts, roughly chopped
1 unbaked pie crust (see page 212)
2 cups heavy cream, lightly whipped

Method

Beat the eggs until they are frothy. Pour in honey and maple syrup, then beat well. Stir in the arrowroot, then fold in the walnuts.

Pour the mixture into the pie shell, and bake in a preheated 375° F. oven for approximately 45 minutes, or until the pie is set.

Remove and let cool. Serve with unflavored whipped cream.

Yield: Six servings

Polenta

This recipe will serve eight as an appetizer or as a potato substitute, or four for lunch. It is delightful accompanied by a green salad with a dressing of sherry wine vinegar, oil, cracked black pepper, and salt.

1/2 pound hot or sweet sausage
1 tablespoon olive oil
4 1/2 cups water
2 tablespoons kosher salt
1 3/4 cups coarsely ground cornmeal
1/2 cup, plus 1 tablespoon unsalted butter
1/2 cup, plus 2 tablespoons grated Gruyère cheese
1/4 pound Gorgonzola cheese
2 grinds black pepper
1/4 cup grana, grated

Method

Remove the sausages from their casings and sauté crumbled, in olive oil.

In a heavy-bottomed pot, bring the water to a rolling boil. Turn down to a simmer, add the salt, and swirl the water with a wooden spoon. Slowly pour the cornmeal into the water in a thin stream, stirring constantly to prevent lumping. As the water fills with cornmeal, pour even more slowly. It is more apt to lump at the end. When all the cornmeal has been added, reduce the heat to very low. Cook gently, stirring often, for about 45 minutes. The mixture will be quite thick.

Remove the pot from the heat and stir in 1/2 cup butter and the Gruyère. Let cool for 30 minutes.

In a buttered baking dish large enough to hold all the ingredients, layer polenta, Gorgonzola, pepper, grana, and sausage meat. Continue layering, ending with polenta. Sprinkle grana over, and dribble with oil.

Bake at 375° F. for about 25 minutes, until browned on the top. Remove. Cool slightly, then cut into pieces like a cake and serve. A light tomato sauce is a fine accompaniment (see page 210).

Yield: Four servings

Chicken Fried in the Southern Style

Two 2 1/2-pound frying chickens, well dried
2   cups whole milk
1 1/2   cups flour
1   teaspoon kosher salt
Black pepper, freshly ground
1   cup light oil, soy or corn oil
1   cup duck or bacon fat

Method
    Cut each chicken into 8 pieces. Place the pieces in the milk to soak for 45 minutes to an hour, turning occasionally.
    Mix the flour with the salt and pepper to taste.
    Remove the chicken from the milk, allowing any excess to run off, and coat it well in the flour. Shake off excess flour.
    Heat the oil in a heavy-bottomed skillet until hot, but not smoking (oil and fat should be 3/4-inch deep in skillet). Place chicken pieces in the skillet. Do not crowd them. Reduce heat to medium, and cook for 4–5 minutes on one side until they are lightly golden. Turn the pieces over and reduce the heat to low. Cover the pan and cook another 10 minutes. Uncover, and turn the pieces once more, letting them cook for an additional 4–5 minutes, or until they are dark golden brown.
    This method will produce a chicken that is moist and tender on the inside with a thin tender crust on the outside. It is delicious accompanied by warm cornbread with jalapeño peppers and perhaps even a garlic cream sauce.

Yield: Four servings

Sausage Toasts with Garlic Cream

Ingredients for the Toast
- 1/2 pound hot or sweet Italian sausages
- 1 tablespoon olive oil
- Four 1/2-inch-thick slices Italian or French bread
- 1 tablespoon unsalted butter
- 1 tablespoon garlic purée or 1 teaspoon fresh garlic, minced

Ingredients for the Sauce
1 tablespoon garlic purée or 1/2 teaspoon fresh garlic, minced
1 teaspoon shallot, chopped
2 tablespoons unsalted butter
1/4 cup dry white wine
1 cup heavy cream
Kosher salt
Black pepper, freshly ground
Parsley leaves, chopped

Method

Remove the sausages from their casing and sauté, crumbled, in the olive oil. Set aside.

Spread the bread slices with the butter, then the garlic purée. Place them in a 400° F. oven for 8 minutes.

While the breads are toasting, sauté the garlic purée and shallots in butter in a small skillet over medium heat for 2–3 minutes, until they begin to turn golden. Add the wine and reduce to about 2 tablespoons liquid. Add the cream. Bring to a high simmer and reduce by about one-third, or until it begins to thicken. Remove the skillet from the heat. Add salt and pepper to taste.

Remove the toast from the oven. Lightly pack them with the sausage and return to the oven. Heat through for approximately 2–3 minutes. Reheat the sauce and put a generous pool in the center of each warmed plate. Float the toast in the middle of each pool, sprinkle with parsley, and serve.

Yield: Four servings

Potato and Leek Soup

The great Paul Bocuse chose to prepare a potato and leek soup for his fiftieth birthday. There is nothing ordinary about this dish.

- 1/2 cup onions, chopped
- 1 cup leeks, white part only, well washed and chopped
- 2 tablespoons unsalted butter
- 1 cup potatoes, peeled and chopped
- 1 teaspoon kosher salt
- 2 cups water
- 2 cups chicken stock (see page 204)
- 1/2–3/4 cup heavy cream
- Ground white pepper to taste
- 1/4 cup fresh chives, chopped
- Black pepper, freshly ground

Method

Melt the onions and leeks in butter until translucent. Stir in the potatoes and salt. Cover, and cook for 4–5 minutes. Add the water and stock and boil gently until the potatoes are quite soft.

Strain. Purée the solids with a little bit of the liquid in a food processor, blender, or food mill. Add the purée to the strained liquid, and stir in the cream.

Return to the heat and bring to a simmer. Taste, and season with salt and white pepper, if necessary.

Ladle the soup into hot bowls and sprinkle with chives and cracked black pepper.

For a cold soup, allow it to cool completely, then refrigerate until cold. Add the cream to the cold mixture and mix well. Serve in well chilled bowls.

Yield: Four servings

Linguiça and Kale Soup

This soup brings back many fond memories of my Portuguese grandmother, who made it often.

- 1/2 cup carrots, thinly sliced
- 1 large onion, sliced
- 1 tablespoon garlic purée or 2–3 cloves garlic, finely chopped
- 2 tablespoons olive oil
- 3/4 pound linguiça or other spicy ethnic sausage like chorizo or Italian pepperoni, sliced in 1/2-inch rounds
- 1 1/2 pounds kale leaves, well washed and chopped
- 4 cups chicken or beef stock (see pages 204, 203)
- 1 bay leaf
- 8 tiny red-skinned potatoes, sliced
- 1 1/2 tablespoons kosher salt
- 1/4 cup grana, finely grated

Method

In a 6-quart pot, gently cook carrots, onion, and garlic in the olive oil until onions are translucent.

Add the linguiça and simmer 5 minutes.

Add the kale and toss it well. Cook 3–4 minutes.

Add stock, bay leaf, potatoes, and salt. Gently simmer about 30 minutes, or until the potatoes are tender.

Ladle into bowls and serve with grated grana on top.

Yield: Four servings

Chapter X

Coulibiac

Ambiance

...all and everything

Cultured Chinese are said to talk only about food at the dinner table. There are no disturbing discussions of politics, religion, or anything else disruptive. There is an aura of calm, conducive to the concentration necessary for savoring the foods.

Many things must be considered to produce a successful dinner. I can say from experience that there is no such thing as absolute consistency, although for a chef it is always the goal. No matter how many times you prepare a particular dish, it is going to vary somewhat. Just as there are differences within meats and vegetables because of where they were grown, when they were picked, the time of year, and the food that the animal or plant was fed, there are myriad influences that modify, thus producing slight variations. These variations are not necessarily bad, in and of themselves. You cannot, to use a theatrical term, "set a piece." You can have consistency only up to a point. Once you understand this, it removes some of the pressure.

Producing the proper ambiance is like staging a play. First you assemble the "cast" of ingredients, then "you learn the 'ography," the recipes and techniques necessary for preparing the dishes, so that you are not grappling with the fundamentals in the middle of the "performance." Then, just as in a theatrical performance, you get "costumed," set your lighting, and assemble your props—dishes, flowers, etc. You have a "curtain time," which is when your first guests arrive. Somewhere in the middle of the second act, or main course, you have your revelatory scene, or high point; then everything slowly diminishes.

Basic to accomplishing this is the thorough understanding of each step, so that they become second nature. All truly great artists, whether a Picasso, a Stravinsky, or a Balanchine, learn classical theory. Once mastered, you have the foundation and freedom to develop your own theories—and from there to go on to new and personal concepts.

Every aspect of an evening is important. The china, silver, crystal, space, and seating arrangements—all must echo the same intention. The overall mood is the "floor" to the evening, a floor upon which the food dances. When City Ballet was about to move into Lincoln Center, Balanchine went numerous times to check the floor that was being laid. He was acutely aware that everything was dependent upon that floor: it had to work properly for the dancers. Similarly, the choice of china, linen, and flowers has to be taken into consideration, along with the food that is going to be served. These elements should not compete with the food. Rather, they must serve as a complementary base.

Ideally, it would be wonderful to have many different kinds of china and crystal to use with the various types of meals that one serves. In reality, most households have but one or two sets of china. There is a physicalness to holding a wine glass—a sensuality in the feel of its stem and the clarity of the crystal. Since the food is of prime importance, I prefer dishes that are as large as possible. They should be elegant, but simple. I generally design the composition as I plate it. It becomes very difficult to design a clean and clear composition around colors and structural elements that are part of the plate.

The same holds true for flowers and linen. They should work as a base, not as competing elements. Flowers should be arranged low enough on the table that they do not impede eye contact. Their fragrance should not quarrel with the aromas of the food. Tuberoses or Easter lilies should be avoided! For example, several "important" flowers can be arranged in a pincushion, the cushion then masked with Spanish moss or black or crystal pebbles.

A plate should never be filled to overflowing. It should not intimidate by the amount of food placed upon it. A steak shouldn't be hanging off the edge; it should be contained or framed by the perimeter of the plate.

Candles add immeasurably to the ambiance of an evening. Their flicker heightens the opalescence of a sauce and the clarity of the wine; and the play of light on the silver or on the wood of the table adds sparkle. They create light and therefore life—visual interest without busyness.

The music for an evening should be sequenced, the way a well-designed concert is sequenced. It should start slowly and build, competing neither with the conversation nor with the food. It should bring people subliminally to a height, toward the end of the evening.

It is important that people have enough space in which to eat. Place settings should not be so crowded that your guests are afraid of knocking over each other's wine glasses.

Seating arrangements require careful attention, especially for more formal parties. The seating plan can generate a balance to the conversation.

Scallop Bisque with Seafood Sausage

One of the most luxurious soups in taste and presentation. When the sausage is first broken with your spoon it almost becomes a blanquette, encompassing all of the sweet flavors of the sea.

    Seafood Sausage (see page 188 and Note)
    Optional: Roe of 1 lobster (from sausage preparation)
    2   tablespoons unsalted butter

Ingredients for Court Bouillon
    1   leek, white part only, well washed
    1/2 cup onion, roughly chopped
    1/2 cup carrots, peeled and thinly sliced
    3   parsley stems
    1   small pinch fennel seed, crushed or ground
    1   bay leaf
    2   cups dry white wine
    2   cups water
    1 1/2 teaspoons kosher salt
    6   black peppercorns

Ingredients for Bisque
    3/4 pound bay or sea scallops
    1   cup heavy cream
    1   pinch cayenne pepper
    1   tablespoon fresh chives, chopped

Method

In a stainless steel saucepan combine all the ingredients for the court bouillon. Gently simmer for 30 minutes. Strain out and discard the solids.

Return the liquid to the pan, and bring to a boil. Add the scallops, and poach for 2 minutes. Strain and set the scallops aside for use in the sausage.

Return the liquid to the pan again. Cook and reduce for 5 minutes. Check the seasoning. The liquid should have a slightly stronger taste than desired in the finished bisque, as the cream will soften the taste. Add the cayenne.

Add the cream and gently simmer for 8–10 minutes.

If the lobster you cooked for the Seafood Sausage contained roe, purée the roe with 2 tablespoons butter to form a lobster butter. Set aside.

If you have made lobster butter, remove the soup from the heat and quickly swirl in the butter. This will change the color to a beautiful coral, as the heat cooks the coral.

Place 2 slices of seafood sausage in the bottom of warmed soup plates. Ladle the soup and sprinkle with fresh chives.

(You may omit the sausage. If you do, chop the scallops and add 1 1/2 tablespoons to each bowl before ladling in the bisque.)

Yield: Four servings

Risotto with White Truffles

Risotto can be served as a first course, as an accompaniment to meat or fowl, or for lunch with a green salad.

1–1 1/2   ounces fresh white truffle
1   cup imported Aborio rice
1/2   cup onion, medium chopped
3   tablespoons soft unsalted butter
3   cups chicken stock (see page 204)
1   carrot
1   leek, white part only
1/2   onion stuck with 2 cloves
3   parsley stems
1   sprig fresh thyme
1/4   cup grana, finely grated
Kosher salt
Black pepper, freshly ground

Method

Place the truffle in the rice, and refrigerate for 3 to 4 days, tightly covered.

Remove the truffle, mince or shave it, and set aside.

Simmer the stock for 45 minutes with the carrot, leek, onion with cloves, parsley stems, and thyme. Set aside.

Cook the chopped onion in 3 tablespoons butter until it is translucent. Stir in the rice and cook for about 4 minutes or until the kernels turn opaque.

Add the strained stock, in 1/2 cup increments, stirring continuously. Do not add more liquid until the previous liquid has been absorbed by the rice. This should take approximately 18 minutes. At this point, the rice should be "al dente" and quite wet. Add more liquid as needed to obtain a desired consistency. Remove from the heat and gently stir in the grana and 2 tablespoons of soft butter. Add the truffle, and season with salt and pepper to taste.

Yield: Four servings

Variations

- Instead of a truffle, stir in 1 cup sliced wild or domestic mushrooms that have been sautéed in 2 tablespoons olive oil and 1 tablespoon butter.
- Mussels: Steam open 2 pounds mussels in 1/2 cup water, 1/2 cup dry white wine, and 1 finely chopped shallot. Drain, reserving the liquid. Strain this liquid through a sieve lined with washed cheesecloth or linen. Add enough liquid to make 3 cups. Use this in place of the chicken stock when cooking the Aborio rice. Remove the mussels from the shells. Stir mussels, grana, 1/4 cup parsley leaves, and 1/2 teaspoon dried oregano. Season to taste with salt.
- Add 3/4 cup diced smoked salmon, 1 ounce good sturgeon caviar, 1/2 cup sour cream, and 1/4 cup chopped parsley.
- Risotto can be dampened with other liquids, such as veal stock or fish fumet, depending upon the dish it is going to accompany.

- Cheeses can also be varied, adding fonduta, fine sharp cheddar, or Gorgonzola.
- Add bits of bacon or Westphalian ham.

Oysters in Garlic Cream with Shallots

Once in my New York restaurant, Odile, a critic laughingly complained to me that his dinner guest was "utterly undone" by this garlic cream sauce.

Since this is an appetizer, use three oysters per person. If you are an oyster lover, then four. If you are an oyster craver, plan on six per person.

    1 tablespoon unsalted butter
    1 medium-size shallot, chopped
    2 medium cloves garlic, very finely chopped or 1 tablespoon garlic purée
    1/4 cup dry white wine
    1 cup heavy cream
    Kosher salt
    12–24 oysters

Method

Place the butter in a small, heavy skillet. When it has melted, add the shallot and garlic. Turn heat to very low and cook gently for approximately 5 minutes. Pay continual attention to make sure they do not brown. This is particularly important, because the slow, gentle cooking of the garlic releases its acrid qualities. It is crucial that the garlic not overpower the other tastes in an oyster dish.

After the garlic and shallot are melted, add the wine. Turn up the heat and reduce the liquid to about 2 tablespoons. Add the cream, and salt to taste. Cook for 4–5 minutes. Lower the heat and add the oysters and their liquids. Cook gently for 1 1/2–2 minutes, until the edges of the oysters start to curl.

With a slotted spoon remove oysters to warmed plates. Return sauce to the heat. Cook until the sauce is medium thick. Check for seasoning, then spoon sauce over the oysters. Pass the peppermill.

Yield: Four servings

Charcuterie Platter

This is a wonderful lunch, light supper, or first course, and it can be put together easily with items that are commercially available. In recent years commercially prepared pâté of good quality has become available. I would suggest preparing a plate with slices of pâté forestière, a duck liver pâté with port wine, some Saucisson de Lyon, sliced pepperoni, warm potato salad (see page 67), a few cornichons, good mustard, and some flavorful compound butters, such as pimento, shallot, or basil butter.

Compound butters are simple to prepare, very colorful, and extremely tasty. They can be packed into crocks and scooped out with a warmed melon baller or teaspoon.

To prepare each butter, use 1/2 cup butter at room temperature. Add 2 tablespoons of finely chopped shallots, chopped pimento, or chopped basil. Incorporate the ingredients into the butter using a food processor or a fork. These compounds are also delightful on simply broiled fish.

Capelli d'Angeli with Salmon and Caviar

6 quarts water
1 cup heavy cream
1 tablespoon shallot, finely chopped
1/2 pound very fresh salmon, all bones and skin removed, cut into 1/2-inch cubes
1/2 pound capelli d'angeli (angel hair pasta)
3 tablespoons kosher salt
3 tablespoons soft unsalted butter
1 ounce fine black caviar (not lump fish caviar)
Black pepper, freshly ground

Method

Because the pasta cooks very rapidly, start the water for the pasta boiling. When it begins to come to a boil, lower the heat and start the sauce.

Put the cream and shallot into a skillet and bring to a gentle simmer. Let the cream reduce slightly and thicken for about 4 minutes. Add the salmon. Continue to gently simmer until salmon is just cooked, 3–4 minutes. Remove from the heat.

Bring the pasta water back to a boil. Add salt. Stir in the pasta. Cook until it is al dente, between 3–5 minutes. Add 1 quart cold water and drain well.

Arrange small mounds of the pasta on well-warmed plates. Return sauce to the heat and bring to a simmer. Remove from the heat and swirl in butter. Then gently, without breaking the eggs, swirl in the caviar.

Add salt if necessary. Spoon over the pasta, and pass the peppermill.

Yield: Four appetizer servings

Seafood Sausage

This is an excellent first course, served in slices on a warm plate, accompanied by either beurre blanc or hollandaise sauce.

> 3/4 pound bay or sea scallops
> One 2 1/2-pound lobster
> One 6- or 7-ounce filet of gray or lemon sole
> 1/2 cup heavy cream
> 1 1/2 teaspoons kosher salt
> 2 tablespoons flat parsley, chopped
> 1/2 pound medium shrimp, cleaned, deveined, and roughly chopped
> 1/4 teaspoon white pepper, ground

Method

If sea scallops are used, slice them into thirds across the grain. Poach the scallops in a court bouillon for 2 minutes (see pages 182, 214). Remove and cool. Reserve the bouillon if you make scallop bisque.

Cook the lobster in boiling water to cover, for 5 minutes. Remove, and cool under running water. Remove the meat. Discard the queen, and reserve the roe (the dark green part of the lobster) if there is any. Roughly chop the lobster meat.

Place the filet of sole in a food processor and purée. Add the cream and salt to the purée and process for 1 minute.

Put the purée and parsley in a bowl. Add the lobster, shrimp, and scallops. Mix well. Season with white pepper.

Spread a long piece of plastic wrap on the table. Spoon a band of seafood mixture down the center, 2 inches wide and 12 inches long. Roll and seal, but do not wrap too tightly, as the mixture will expand as it cooks. Tie both ends tight with butcher's twine. The ingredients should make 2 sausages.

Poach in simmering water for 10–12 minutes.

Yield: Two entrée or four appetizer portions

Lace Tulip Cookies

These cookies can be used as a container for mousse, sorbet, or fresh fruit.

- 1 cup finely ground blanched almonds
- 3/4 cup sugar
- 6 tablespoons unsalted butter
- 4 teaspoons unbleached flour, sifted
- 2 tablespoons milk

Method

Combine and mix all the ingredients into a smooth paste. (This is most easily done in a food processor.)

Cover a cookie sheet with baking parchment cut into 6-inch squares. These cookies spread considerably, so by making individual sheets for them to rest on in the pan, it is easier to remove them after baking.

Place a large tablespoon of batter on each paper. Wet your fingers with water and push and spread the batter into a 3-inch circle. Leave a lot of space around the cookies, as they will spread to between 5 and 6 inches each. Bake in a preheated 350° F. oven for about 12 minutes, until they are gold and riddled with holes.

Remove from the oven and cool for 1 minute. Working quickly, gently remove each cookie from the pan and mold it over the bottom of an inverted custard cup or muffin tin. Make sure that the center of the cookie is pressed down to form a flat bottom. Let them cool in position for 4–5 minutes, then remove and store in an airtight container.

You can prepare the batter a day in advance and refrigerate it, but let the batter come to room temperature before baking.

Yield: About 12 cookies

Polenta with Sausage, Chicken, and Tomato Sauce

1 small chicken, cut up, or 2 1/2–3 pounds of chicken parts
3 tablespoons olive oil
Polenta (see page 171)
Tomato sauce (see page 210)
1 1/2 pounds Italian hot or sweet sausage
Kosher salt
Black pepper to taste
1/2 cup grated grana
2 tablespoons flat parsley leaves, roughly chopped

Method

Lightly brown the chicken pieces in the olive oil. Set aside.

Form the prepared polenta into a large flattened mound with a crater in the center, made by pressing down with the back of a large spoon. The mound should be formed on an ovenproof platter, with an edge that can contain the sauce of the finished dish.

Submerge the chicken pieces in the tomato sauce and gently simmer for 25 minutes. Place the polenta in the oven at 375° F. when you set the tomato sauce to cook, so that it cooks for about 25–30 minutes. Add the sausages to the sauce, and simmer for the last 12–15 minutes.

Using a slotted spoon, place the pieces of chicken and sausage in the crater of the polenta. Pour the sauce over, and sprinkle liberally with parsley.

Bring the dish to the table, and allow each person to serve themselves. Pass the grana and the peppermill.

Yield: Four to six servings

Lobster Toast

1 bay leaf
2 sprigs fresh thyme or 1/4 teaspoon dried thyme
6 whole black peppercorns
1 leek, white part only
1 loaf dense white bread, unsliced
One 2-pound lobster
6 tablespoons unsalted butter
2 tablespoons soy oil
1 carrot, grated
1 tablespoon shallot, chopped
2 tablespoons cognac
1/2 cup dry white wine
3/4 cup fish fumet (see page 202)
3/4 cup heavy cream
Kosher salt
1/4 cup grana, grated
Black pepper, freshly ground

Method

Tie the bay leaf, thyme, peppercorns, and leek in a cheesecloth bag to form a bouquet garni. Set aside.

Cut the bread into four 2 1/2-inch thick slices. Trim off all the crusts. With a small sharp knife, make a hollow in each cube of bread, leaving a 1/2-inch-thick wall all around. These cubes will encase the lobster.

Plunge the lobster into rapidly boiling salted water. Cook for 5 minutes. Cool, and remove the meat. Cut it into small pieces.

Heat 2 tablespoons of the butter and 1 tablespoon of oil in a pan over high heat. Add the lobster meat and toss well for 2 minutes. With a slotted spoon, remove the lobster to a side dish.

Lower the heat and add another tablespoon of butter. Sauté the carrot and shallots until the shallots are translucent.

Remove the pan from the heat, averting your face, add the cognac. Put out the flame with a cover. Then add the wine, fish fumet, and bouquet garni. Return to the heat, and reduce to about 1 cup.

Strain the mixture, and return the liquid to the pan. Add the heavy cream and salt to taste. Continue to reduce until there is about 1 cup of slightly thickened liquid. Remove from the heat and let cool.

Carefully brush the outside surfaces of the bread squares with approximately 2 tablespoons butter. Turn the cubes upside down on a cookie sheet and bake at 400° F. for 8–10 minutes, until lightly golden. Be sure they don't get too dark, because another cooking process must take place.

Just before you serve the toast, divide the lobster meat among the 4 bread squares. Check the seasoning in the sauce and add salt, if necessary. Pour the sauce over the lobster meat, and fill to the top. Sprinkle with grated grana and lightly dot with butter. Place on a cookie sheet and bake at 450° F. for about 8 minutes, until the top is lightly bubbling and browned. Serve on a warm plate.

Yield: Four servings

Pheasant with a Compote of Pineapple Quince, Artichoke Hearts, and Chestnuts

Ingredients for Compote
- 6 tiny artichokes
- 3/4 cup water
- 1/2 lemon
- 1 pineapple quince
- 8 fresh chestnuts
- 1 1/4 cups chicken stock (see page 204)
- 1 teaspoon white wine vinegar
- 1 small pinch celery seed
- 1 teaspoon garlic purée

Ingredients for Pheasant
>One 2-pound pheasant
>Large pinch kosher salt
>1 pinch black pepper, coarsely ground
>1 teaspoon garlic purée or 1 clove garlic, finely chopped
>4–5 sprigs fresh thyme, leaves removed from the stem and bruised, or 1/4 teaspoon dried thyme
>2 1/2 tablespoons unsalted butter
>Two slices double-smoked bacon, or another fine bacon

Ingredients for Sauce
>1 sprig fresh thyme
>1/4 cup cream
>1 tablespoon cognac

Method

Prepare compote before the bird is roasted.

Pull off all the outer leaves of the artichokes. Cut the stem off 1/4 inch from the base, and cut off the top tips. Peel and trim off all the remaining dark green. As they are prepared, put the artichokes in the water with the juice of half a lemon (acidulated water). This will prevent the artichokes from turning brown. Drain the artichokes, and cook them in simmering salted water to cover until the base is easily pierced. Drain and set aside.

Cut the quince into quarters and remove the core. Place it in a pan with water to cover. Simmer until tender but not soft. Drain. Set aside to cool.

With a sharp knife cut an X on the flat side of the chestnuts' skin. Bake on a cookie sheet in a 300° F. oven until the cuts begin to curl back. Remove and allow them to slightly cool. Peel.

Gently simmer the chestnuts in 3/4 cup of chicken stock until they are tender, about 25 minutes. Add the artichoke hearts and cook for about 2 minutes. Remove the skin from the quince, cut it into fairly large cubes, and add to the chestnut mixture. Add the wine vinegar, celery seed, and garlic purée. Cook for 5 minutes and keep warm over a low flame.

Into the cavity of the pheasant put the salt, pepper, garlic purée, thyme, and butter. Pierce a hole in the skin on either side of the cavity. Cross one leg over and put it through the hole. Repeat on the other side, closing the bird. Lay the bacon slabs over the breast, and place the pheasant breast up on a rack in a roasting pan in a preheated 450° F. oven. Cook for about 45 minutes. Remove the bacon for the last 5 minutes, so that the breasts can take color.

Remove from oven and keep warm.

Drain the juice from the bird and strain it into a small saucepan. Skim off most of the fat. Add the remaining chicken stock and a sprig of thyme. Bring to a boil and reduce by half. Add the cream and boil for about 1 1/2 minutes. Add the cognac and simmer 1 minute.

Carve the pheasant and arrange on warmed plates. Place a spoonful of compote to the side. Spoon the sauce over the pheasant, and serve.

Yield: Two servings

Coulibiac

Any preparation in brioche is an event.

I am including this recipe because I have a particular fondness for it. I believe I was perhaps the first person in Manhattan to prepare coulibiac to be sold over the counter, as take-out. When I began working on the dish I understood how important it was to make sure that the ingredients, particularly the brioche, were cold enough. So I literally put on a hat and coat, in the middle of the summer, and worked in the walk-in refrigerator of my restaurant. As I became more confident in preparing coulibiac, I realized, thank God, that there are other ways to achieve the same results—without freezing to death. The three funnels that are placed in the top of the coulibiac to vent it, along with the expansion of the brioche dough, made me think I had the *Queen Mary* in the oven when I opened the oven door the first time I prepared it.

This is a rather involved recipe, but you can facilitate it by preparing several of the elements in advance.

Coulibiac should be brought to the table whole, but it can be cut into 1-inch-thick slices and served on plates from the kitchen. Traditionally this dish is wonderful when served with a nicely seasoned, hot, clear fish broth, in individual cups, with shots of ice-cold vodka. George Balanchine gave very specific instructions on the way to eat coulibiac. He said:

> "First you have coulibiac,
>   then broth,
>   then vodka,
>   then coulibiac,
>   then broth,
>   then vodka."

Brioche dough (see page 211) (This must be prepared the day before.)
24 crêpes (see page 213) (Can be prepared in advance. Make approximately 24 crêpes)
Velouté (see page 206) (Can be prepared in advance)

Ingredients for the Filling

- 2 pounds center-cut salmon, all skin and bones removed
- 2 teaspoons black pepper, freshly ground
- Kosher salt
- 2 tablespoons fresh dill, chopped
- 1/2 pound fresh mushrooms, thinly sliced
- 2 cups fish velouté (see page 206)
- 2 cups cooked wild rice, well seasoned (see page 215)
- 3 hard-boiled eggs
- 1 tablespoon minute tapioca
- 1/2 cup water
- 2 pounds spinach leaves, heavy stems removed, cooked until just wilted
- 1/2 cup butter, melted

Ingredients for Brioche Glaze
    2   egg yolks
    3   tablespoons water

Method

Prepare the fish at least 4 hours in advance of the final assembly.

Lay each salmon filet horizontally on a cutting board and cut 1-inch slices as you would London broil, at a 30-degree angle.

In a shallow stainless steel, glass, or enamel baking pan, about 12 by 8 inches, place the salmon in two long rows with each piece overlapping, forming a shingle pattern. Sprinkle liberally with black pepper, a little salt, and dill. Spread the mushrooms over, completely covering the salmon. Gently pour velouté sauce over the salmon and mushrooms, smooth the surface with a spatula, and allow the mixture to cool completely. Cover with plastic wrap and refrigerate for 4 hours minimum.

Put the prepared rice in a bowl. Press the hard boiled eggs through a sieve into the rice. In a small pan, sprinkle the tapioca into 1/2 cup water and allow it to dissolve. Gently warm it, to make sure that it dissolves completely. Pour this into the rice and egg mixture, and mix well. Taste for salt and pepper. (The tapioca is a substitute for vesiga—sturgeon marrow—which is available here in dried form, but is very difficult and time-consuming to reconstitute.)

Assembly: On a lightly floured board, roll the brioche dough to a 5/8-inch thickness. Trim the dough to measure 20 inches long and 14 inches wide. Save the trimmings. Transfer the dough to a large lightly floured cookie sheet. Place 6–8 of the crêpes down the length of the dough in the center, beginning 2 inches from the top and ending approximately 2 inches from the bottom. The crêpes should be arranged in pairs, slightly overlapping. Then make an island of wild rice on top, approximately 5 inches wide, 14 inches long, and 1/2 inch thick. With a long spatula lift off as many as you can of the salmon shingles in one scoop. Place them upside down on the rice. Repeat, until one strip of shingles has been used and all the rice is covered. Lightly spread the spinach over the surface. Lay down another layer of 6–8 crêpes on top of the spinach. Arrange the remainder of the salmon shingles on top of the spinach, mushroom side up. Pack the remainder of the wild rice on top, then cover with another layer of 6–8 crepes.

Mix the egg yolks with 3 tablespoons water. Bring one long side of the brioche dough up and over the top of the loaf. Paint the top of the dough with this egg wash, then bring the other side up and over the painted area. Using the egg wash as a glue, seal by gently pressing the dough together. Paint the two end flaps with egg wash and fold upward to seal.

Take another cookie sheet, exactly the same size as the one the dough is on, and butter the surface. Place it over the loaf, and invert quickly, so that the seam of the brioche is lying flat on the bottom of the buttered pan.

On the top of the brioche, with a sharp knife, cut and remove three small circles or diamond shapes, one in the center and the other two equidistant from the center. Form tiny funnels with aluminum foil and place these into the holes. They will permit the steam to escape, and prevent the liquid from oozing down the sides of the loaf.

Paint the entire surface of the brioche with the remaining egg wash. At this time the scrap pieces of brioche dough can be formed into shapes and stuck to the brioche with egg wash, then also painted.

Bake in a preheated 425° F. oven for 10 minutes. Lower the heat to 375° F. and continue to bake for an additional 50 minutes. Check and turn the pan after 30 minutes to ensure even browning. If the top of the brioche is browning too rapidly, place a sheet of aluminum foil over it.

The coulibiac is done when it is a golden brown and the internal temperature is 115–120° F. Remove from the oven and let it rest for 10–15 minutes.

Just before serving, melt the butter. Pour equal amounts down through the funnels so that it is taken into the entire loaf. Remove funnels and serve.

Yield: Four to six servings

Chapter XI

The Ingredients for Mayonnaise

Basic Preparations

...simple, but not easy

Basic preparations, such as beurre blanc, hollandaise, wild rice, and steamed spinach, are important elements in and of themselves as well as being key ingredients in other dishes. At first glance they seem very easy to prepare because there are few ingredients and preparation time is frequently short. One or two preparation techniques are crucial to the success of these recipes. Having these basics in your repertoire will greatly add to your ability to prepare many dishes and to expand your own creativity.

Fish Fumet

    5 pounds heads, tails, and trimmings from white-fleshed fish, such as halibut, red snapper, haddock, sole, or flounder
    Water to cover, about 4 quarts

Method

Rinse the bones well in cold water. Remove the gills from the fish heads to prevent them from releasing solids. Place the fish in a noncorrosive pot, cover with water, and bring to a simmer. Skim well. Allow to simmer for 20 minutes. Remove from the heat and strain through a very fine sieve, or a sieve lined with three thicknesses of washed cheesecloth or linen.

Yield: Four quarts

Fish Stock without Fish

While the finest fish stocks are prepared with the heads and tails of fresh fish, there are many places in the United States where fresh fish are not readily available. I have found that a suitable substitute can be prepared by soaking 1/2 cup Japanese shaved, dried bonito flakes in 2 cups warm water. Simmer for 2–3 minutes and strain.

Yield: 2 cups

Beef-Veal Stock

　　4　pounds veal bones, preferably in 2–3-inch lengths to maximize the release of marrow
　　2　pounds beef shin bone, with some meat still clinging
　　1　pound beef trimmings, such as trimmings from pot roast
　　4　cups cold water

Method

　　Place the bones and meat in one layer in a roasting pan. If there is too much to be contained in one pan, divide it between two. To turn deep brown, the bones should be only one layer deep. Roast at 400° F. for 1 1/2 hours, turning every 15 minutes after the first 30 minutes.

　　Remove from oven and place in a stockpot, leaving the fat behind. Cover with cold water by 2 inches.

　　Pour off fat. Deglaze with a little water. Add to stockpot.

　　Bring to a simmer on top of the stove. At the point it reaches a simmer, pour in 2 cups cold water to ensure the proper temperature for the release of the albumin from the meat. Skim, then repeat the process, adding 2 cups cold water before the next simmer. Then skim. Make sure the surface of the liquid is always well cleaned. Never boil. Gently simmer for 8–10 hours.

　　Remove from the stove, cool slightly, and strain. Return the stock to the pot, bring to a boil, and remove the final traces of fat from the surface. Reduce by about half. Cool and store.

　　Can be refrigerated, tightly sealed. If it is brought to a boil every three days, allowed to cool, and refrigerated again, it lasts for weeks.

Yield:　2 quarts

Chicken Stock

    1   soup chicken: an older, larger bird, too tough for sautéeing or broiling
    5   quarts water

Always use an older bird when available. While it is not as tender, it is full of flavor. Cut it into pieces and put them, including the neck, into a pot with cold water. Bring to a simmer, add 1 cup of cold water, and skim the scum and fat carefully. Repeat this process of adding water and skimming. Adding the water lowers the temperature so that the flesh can continue releasing its natural albumin. *Never* let the stock boil, because boiling homogenizes the fats into the stock. Repeat the skimming process approximately 3 times. Allow to simmer gently for 4 hours.

When the stock is finished, strain the stock through frozen cheesecloth. Freezing maximizes the number of small particles of fat that will adhere to the cheesecloth.

Cool completely, and store.

Can be stored refrigerated for three or four days.

Yield: 1 gallon

Glace de Viande

Reduce the beef-veal stock (see page 203) by two-thirds.

Glace means glaze. This is a heavy reduction, to evaporate the water and concentrate the marrow qualities of the stock.

Rémoulade Sauce

    1   cup mayonnaise (see page 208)
    1   anchovy, mashed
    1   teaspoon capers
    1   teaspoon garlic purée (see page 217)
    5   cornichons, roughly chopped

Method

Combine all the ingredients and blend well.

Yield: 1 cup

Salsa

    1/2   medium onion, chopped
    2   medium tomatoes, peeled and chopped, or 3 Italian-style plum tomatoes, chopped
    1   fresh or 1 jarred jalapeño pepper
Juice of 1/2 lime
    2   teaspoons garlic purée or 1 clove garlic, roughly chopped
Kosher salt
    2   sprigs fresh oregano leaves, or 1/2 teaspoon dried oregano
Optional: 1 teaspoon fresh cilantro, chopped

Method

Combine onions and tomatoes.

Add the jalapeño, lime juice, and garlic. Season to taste with salt.

Stir in the oregano, and cilantro, if you are using it. Let sit for 1 hour, until the flavors marry. This sauce is best when used fresh.

Yield: 1 1/4 cups

Velouté

3   tablespoons unsalted butter
4   tablespoons flour
2 1/2   cups fish fumet (see page 202)
Kosher salt
Ground white pepper

Method

In a heavy-bottomed stainless steel saucepan, melt the butter over low heat. Stir in the flour and let it cook on low heat while stirring constantly for 2 minutes. It should not brown at all. Remove from the heat and cool for 1 minute.

In another pan, bring the fumet to the boiling point. Pour it all at once into the flour mixture and beat with a wire whisk to fully combine the ingredients.

Place the pan back on the heat and raise the flame to medium. While stirring constantly, bring the mixture to a boil and let it continue to boil for 2 minutes. Remove from the heat. Add salt and white pepper to taste.

It can be used at this point or it can be set aside to completely cool.

The sauce has a tendency to form a skin. To prevent this, take a piece of butter and move it around the top to form a thin butter film.

Do not store the velouté until it is completely cooled, and do not store it for more than 2 days.

Before using after refrigeration, gently heat it while stirring continuously. If it becomes too thick, it may be thinned with fish fumet or cream.

Yield: 2 1/2 cups

Hollandaise Sauce

2   egg yolks
Juice of 1/4 lemon
1/2   teaspoon kosher salt
1   small pinch cayenne pepper
1   tablespoon water
1   cup unsalted butter, clarified

Method

Put the yolks in a stainless steel bowl. Add the lemon juice, salt, and water. Whisk until mixture is lemon yellow and frothy.

Place the pan over, *not in,* gently simmering water. Whisk continuously until mixture is slightly thickened and the whisk is tracing lines in the bottom of the bowl. Remove from the heat immediately. Continue to beat for 30 to 40 seconds to lightly cool the mixture.

Add butter slowly while constantly whisking. It is very important to add the butter slowly, to allow eggs to completely absorb the butter. Add the cayenne pepper.

Place over very warm water, or near a very gentle heat, until further use is required.

Yield: 1 1/4 cups

Mayonnaise

    1   egg, at room temperature
    2   egg yolks, at room temperature
    1   tablespoon freshly squeezed lemon juice
    1   teaspoon kosher salt
    2 3/4   cups light oil
    1/4   cup *fine* olive oil

Method

Place the eggs in a medium bowl. Warm them to slightly more than room temperature by placing the bowl in a pot of warm water. This increases the eggs' ability to take in the oil.

Beat the eggs with the lemon juice and salt until they are thick and a light lemon color. Slowly add the oils in a thin stream, beating continuously, until the mayonnaise is creamy and has taken all the oil. The mayonnaise should be the consistency of vanilla pudding before it is cooled and should jiggle in the bowl. If it becomes too thick, beat in increments of 1/2 teaspoons of water until the correct consistency is achieved. Taste for seasoning.

A myriad of ingredients can be added to this basic mayonnaise to produce variations.

Variations

- Aioli: Stir through a tablespoon of garlic purée (see page 217). Reduce the lemon juice by half and add 1 tablespoon white, red, or sherry wine vinegar.
- Add 1/4 cup nicely browned diced bacon bits. Add an herb of your choice.
- Add 1/4 cup of fine grana, grated.

Author's Note on Mayonnaise

It is difficult to scale down this recipe because there is a need for a minimum egg mass, to incorporate the oil. This recipe yields approximately 3 cups of mayonnaise. It may be stored refrigerated for 1 week. Its flavor does change slightly after 3 days.

Yield: 3 cups

Beurre Blanc

The success of this recipe is absolutely dependent upon an understanding of the change that takes place in the butter with the addition of heat. While it may appear to be a very simple recipe, it is one that intimidates many of the finest chefs, so it shouldn't be taken lightly. It requires the cook's complete attention during its relatively short preparation.

- 1/4 cup dry white wine
- 1 tablespoon vinegar
- 1 teaspoon shallot, chopped
- 2 tablespoons cold water
- 1 cup butter, very cold, cut into tablespoon-size pieces
- 1/4 teaspoon kosher salt

Method

In a heavy-bottomed, noncorrosive saucepan, combine white wine, vinegar, and shallots. Then over moderate heat, reduce to a marmalade.

Remove from the heat and add 2 tablespoons of cold water to cool the pan. The bottom of the pan should have become quite hot by the time it becomes a marmalade. The water will bring the heat down quickly, so that the butter will not break. This is absolutely *crucial* to the success of the sauce. Then swirl the butter in quickly, two pieces at a time at the beginning, to further cool the pan, then 1 piece after another when the sauce begins to "take," until all the pieces have been added. Once the sauce has lost some of its heat, it can be put back on the burner. At that point even a slight bubbling at the edges will not break the sauce. Add salt.

Yield: 1 cup

Tomato Sauce

Optional: 1 tablespoon garlic purée or 2 cloves garlic, minced
1/2 cup onion, roughly chopped
1 medium carrot, roughly grated
1/4 cup olive oil
5–6 fresh tomatoes, peeled, seeded, and chopped, or 1 large can Italian-style plum tomatoes, drained and chopped
1 tablespoon kosher salt
Black pepper
8 fresh basil leaves, roughly torn, or 1/2 teaspoon dried basil

Method

In a stainless steel pot large enough to hold all the ingredients, melt the garlic (if you are using it), onion, and carrot in the olive oil for about 10–12 minutes.

Add the tomatoes and increase the heat to a high simmer. Simmer for about 20 minutes.

Remove from heat and add salt, pepper, and basil. Mix well and taste for seasoning. If the sauce is too thin, continue to simmer, uncovered, until desired consistency is reached.

Can be refrigerated, well covered, for two days.

Yield: 2 cups

Brioche Dough

This preparation must be made the day before it is used.

- 1 tablespoon sugar
- 3/4 cup milk, warmed
- 3 packages dry yeast
- 4–5 cups unbleached and unbromated flour, such as Hecker's or King Arthur
- 2 teaspoons kosher salt
- 6 egg yolks
- 3 whole eggs
- 1 cup very soft unsalted butter

Method

Stir the sugar into warm milk. Sprinkle the yeast over the top and set aside to allow the yeast to develop.

Sift together 4 cups of flour with the salt.

Add the milk mixture, egg yolks, and whole eggs to the sifted flour. Stir the ingredients until they form a dough. Add butter and stir it in well. The dough should be fairly soft and quite sticky at this point.

Turn the dough out onto a heavily floured board or surface, and begin to knead in small amounts of the remaining cup of flour as the dough will take it. Continue to knead for 8–10 minutes, until the dough becomes smooth, elastic, and the surface begins to show blisters.

Place the dough in a bowl and sprinkle lightly with additional flour. Cover the bowl with a clean towel, and leave it in a draft-free, warm area until it doubles in size. Punch the dough down. Form it into a ball and cover again. Let it rise again until it doubles in size. Again this will take about 1 1/2 hours, depending on the room temperature. Punch down again, form a ball, and place a cover on the dough. Then weight the top heavily to keep the dough pressed down. Place the bowl, covered and weighted, in a large plastic bag, or wrap in plastic wrap, to make sure that it is airtight. Place this in the coldest part of the refrigerator overnight, or for a minimum of 8 hours.

Yield: Sufficient dough for Coulibiac

Pastry Dough

- 2 cups unbleached flour
- 4 tablespoons sugar
- 1/4 teaspoon kosher salt
- 7 tablespoons unsalted butter, very cold, cut into equal pieces
- 1 egg yolk
- 1/4 cup cold water

Method

Sift flour, sugar, and salt together.

Cut the butter into the dry ingredients with a food processor, or by hand with a pastry cutter. Add the egg yolk and water to the mixture. Mix just until it forms a ball.

Put the dough on a lightly floured marble slab, Formica top, or other cool smooth surface. *Frissage* the dough by taking the heel of your hand and pushing small amounts of dough outward, to the edge of the surface. Form the dough into a ball again. Wrap in plastic wrap and refrigerate for 1 hour.

It is important that the butter not soften, because it will prevent the dough from being workable.

Remove dough from the refrigerator. On a lightly floured surface, roll it out to an 8-inch circle. Fold the left side over the center, the right side over the left, the top down over the center, and the bottom over it. This folding helps lock air in, as you do with puff pastry, and therefore makes the dough flakier. Turn the dough over. Roll out to 3/16-inch thickness. Trim the dough to size and put it into tart or pie pans. Put the pan in the freezer to set. This prevents the sides or the bottom from falling or bubbling.

Bake 10–12 minutes at 475° F. until pale brown, if another preparation is to take place. Bake until golden brown if not to be baked again.

Dough can be made in advance and frozen in plastic wrap.

Yield: Two single crusts, or approximately sixteen tarts

Crêpes

1   cup cold water
1   cup cold milk
2   cups sifted flour
4   eggs
1/2 teaspoon kosher salt
1   tablespoon parsley, chopped
1   tablespoon fresh dill, chopped
1/4 cup unsalted butter, melted

Method
Put all the ingredients except the butter into a food processor or electric mixer. Process until all the ingredients are thoroughly blended. Add the butter in a thin stream and mix well. The consistency should be that of heavy cream. Let the batter rest for 20 minutes. Quickly fry the crêpes in clarified butter.

Can be stored for two days, tightly sealed.

Yield: Thirty-six 7-inch crêpes

Cornbread

    1 1/2 cups milk
    1   egg
    2   tablespoons light oil
    1   cup white stone-ground cornmeal
    1   cup yellow stone-ground cornmeal
    4   teaspoons baking powder
    1 1/2 teaspoons kosher salt

Method

    Combine the wet ingredients in one bowl.

    Combine the dry ingredients in another bowl. Stir them together and pour into two 8- or 9-inch oiled skillets, which have been heated to hot on top of the stove. Place in a 450° F. oven for about 15 minutes, until golden brown.

Yield: Six servings

Poaching

Poaching is a gentle application of heat. Successful poaching depends on the liquid never boiling. It should only gently shiver.

    The liquid can be various things: a stock of the nature of what you are poaching, such as fish fumet for fish, chicken stock for chicken, or a combination of water and wine.

    Timing is difficult to specify. It must be checked frequently with a thin-bladed knife. When poaching fish, if the blade pierces the flesh with little resistance, the fish is done. If it gets to the point that the flesh flakes, it has already overcooked. Many cookbooks specify flaking as a test for doneness, but the internal heat of the fish will continue to cook it further after it has been removed from the heat; therefore, that cannot serve as a benchmark.

Poaching can also take place in a 325° F. oven, uncovered.

Fresh Pasta

1 3/4 cups unbleached flour
2 large eggs
3 teaspoons milk

Method

Place flour, eggs, and milk in a food processor. Mix until it forms a ball.

Wrap the dough in plastic wrap and refrigerate for an hour.

Roll out the dough as thin as possible. If you use a machine, roll to the next-to-the-last setting. Cut into whatever shape is required.

Yield: Four servings

Wild Rice

1 cup wild rice, rinsed in cold water
4 tablespoons unsalted butter
1 teaspoon kosher salt
Black pepper, freshly ground

Method

Put the rice in a pot and cover with water by 1/2 inch. Bring to a boil. Immediately lower to a gentle simmer. Cover tightly and simmer for 30–35 minutes. Check for doneness. If the rice is not open and cooked, check the liquid. Add a little more liquid, if necessary, cover, and simmer until tender. Remove from heat. Stir in butter, salt, and pepper to taste.

Yield: Four servings

Spinach

2   tablespoons unsalted butter
2   pounds fresh spinach, well washed, stems removed
Kosher salt

Method

Melt the butter in a skillet over medium-high heat until it begins to brown. Add the spinach with water still clinging to it. Sprinkle with a large pinch of salt. Cover quickly, and let it steam for 2–3 minutes, until just wilted. Drain well before serving.

Yield: Four servings

Garlic Purée

Garlic purée gives you "instant garlic." It can be used in any recipe that calls for fresh garlic. Prepare more than is needed for a particular recipe, because it can be kept in the refrigerator for future use. There is a considerable shelf life under refrigeration as long as the purée is sealed with a clear oil, such as a fine olive, soy, or corn oil.

Put the whole bulbs of garlic, without any preparation, on a piece of aluminum foil and wrap them air tight. Make sure there are no holes in the aluminum foil, because the garlic must steam. Holes will permit dry heat to enter the packet, changing the flavor. Place in a 350° F. oven and cook for approximately 45 minutes. Do not let the oven get warmer than 350° F. since increased heat will change the flavor of the garlic.

The garlic can be tested by squeezing the packet to see if it yields. It should be soft.

Remove the packet from the oven and let it cool, still sealed. When cool enough to handle, remove the garlic from the aluminum foil.

With a sharp knife, using a short, rapid sawing motion, cut off the root end of the garlic about 1/4 inch up from the bottom. Be careful not to *press down* on the knife, as that will crush some of the cloves of garlic. Then hold the garlic at the top and press and squeeze the entire bulb, gently moving your fingers forward as you would with a pastry tube or a tube of toothpaste. The garlic cloves should come out of their skins all at the same time, if properly cooked.

Press the garlic through a coarse wire sieve to remove any filaments that were missed. Then mash the garlic with a fork and a little bit of olive or soy oil, or purée it in a food processor with a small amount of olive or soy oil.

Place the purée in a storage container and seal with a 1/4-inch layer of clear oil.

Refrigerate.

Garlic Croûtons

Take 1/2-inch-thick slices of good Italian, French, or homemade white bread. Spread liberally with garlic purée (see page 217), and cut into rounds or cubes, depending upon use. Sauté in a mixture of 1 tablespoon light oil, such as corn or soy oil, and 1 tablespoon fine olive oil.

For a less oily croûton, lightly drizzle the croûtons with olive oil and butter.

Place on a cookie sheet and bake at 425° F. for 8–10 minutes.

Crème Fraîche

2 cups heavy cream
1 cup sour cream

Method

In a saucepan, stir together the cream and sour cream. Place over low heat to take the chill off, but make sure that it never gets more than warm.

It is a very delicate culture that causes the cream to thicken; if the heat gets too high, the culture will die and the process will not be successful.

Pour the slightly warmed ingredients into a very clean container and partially cover it. Leave at room temperature for 6 to 8 hours, or overnight.

An alternative method is to put the cream mixture in a commercial yogurt maker and follow the manufacturer's instructions for yogurt.

Cover, and refrigerate the mixture. Crème fraîche will keep for 1–2 weeks.

Yield: 3 cups

Meringue

2   egg whites
1   tiny pinch kosher salt
1/2   teaspoon freshly squeezed lemon juice
1   pinch cream of tartar (use only if the egg whites are not beaten in a copper bowl)
4   tablespoons sugar

Method

Combine the egg whites, salt, and lemon juice in a copper bowl. Add the cream of tartar if a copper bowl is not used.

Place the bowl in warm water and stir for 1–2 minutes to warm the eggs. Remove the bowl from the warm water and beat the mixture with a whisk or an electric balloon-type mixer. Beat slowly at first, then gradually increase the speed as the whites begin to take air. When they begin to hold soft peaks, sprinkle with the sugar, 1 tablespoon at a time. Beat well after each addition. Continue to beat until the mixture forms firm peaks and becomes shiny.

The meringue may be spooned or piped onto a parchment-lined cookie sheet, forming the shapes that you wish, and dried out in a very slow oven, 175° F. for 2–2 1/2 hours, checking after 1 hour to make sure that they are not taking color. They should remain as white as possible.

Yield: Ten meringues, 2-inch size, or enough to cover 4 brioches

Glossary

ACIDULATED WATER: Water to which a natural acid, such as lemon juice, has been added to retard oxidation and discoloration of certain fruits and vegetables.

BREAK: The improper amalgamation of a sauce due to incorrect preparation or "divine intervention" causing it to separate.

BUTTERFLY: To split down the center, without severing into two parts.

CHIFFONADE: Cutting method by which leaf vegetables or herbs are cut into thin strands, such as a chiffonade of lettuce or basil.

DEGLAZE: Adding a liquid, usually wine or cognac, to a pan which has been used to sauté, in order to take up browned particles on the bottom, thereby adding flavor.

DOLLOP: A large spoonful.

EGG WASH: Mixture of egg yolk and water. Used to seal dough, or painted on to give shine and color to baked goods, such as brioche.

GRANA: An aged grainy cheese (Parmesan, Pecorino Romano, Locatelli), very low in water content and extraordinary in flavor!

INFUSION: The steeping of an element in a liquid so that the element will flavor the liquid; for example, tea and coffee.

Monter au Beurre: To mount with butter, or adding cold butter to a hot liquid to give it viscosity, flavor, and shine.

Pinch: Two fingers full.

Large pinch: Three fingers full.

Pink: Preliminary phase of cooking shrimp, in which the outside has just turned pink and the inside is still raw.

Queen: The sac at the top of the lobster's head. It should be removed.

Strain: Do initial straining through a large sieve to remove the large pieces. Subsequent straining should be done through a fine sieve or cloth. When straining a liquid, always rinse cheesecloth or linen in cold water first to remove sizing or bleach.

Sugar syrup: A syrup composed of water and sugar, often used when a dissolved sugar is necessary.

Index

Aioli Sauce, 208
Almond Paste, 48
Anchovies, 82
   Putanesca Sauce, 164
   Remoulade Sauce, 205
   Steak Tartare, 87
Appetizers: Artichoke Ragoût, 7
   Asparagus, Westphalian Ham, and Pasta with Chèvre Sauce, 69
   Asparagus Maltaise, 6
   Beignets, Savory, 126
   Brie Italienne, 103
   Capelli d'Angeli with Salmon and Caviar, 187
   Carpaccio, 113
   Charcuterie Platter, 186
   Crown of Shrimp, 147
   Duck Livers with Sherry Wine Vinegar, 90
   Fifth Avenue Oysters, 5
   Herb Toast, 51
   Oysters in Garlic Cream with Shallots, 185
   Pizza Turnovers, 53
   Polenta, 171
   Sausage Toasts with Garlic Cream, 173
   Seafood Sausage, 188
   Snails in Garlic Cream, 49
   spinach and oysters on French bread, 104
   Steak Tartare, 87, 104
   Vegetable Curry with Hot Tortilla Chips, 123
Apricots: apricot glaze, 49
   Wild Rice and Hazelnuts with, 35
Artichokes: Artichoke Ragoùt, 7
   Pheasant with Compote of Pineapple Quince, Chestnuts and, 192
Asparagus: Asparagus Maltaise, 6

Double-Baked Potato and Leek Soufflé, 30
Westphalian Ham and Pasta with Chèvre Sauce and, 69
Avocado, Sparrows' Tongues (Linguine) with Salsa and, 23

Bacon: Double-Baked Potato and Leek Soufflé, 30
   Herb Toast, 52
   Parboiled Sautéed Potatoes, 50
   Potato Salad with Garlic, Grana, and Double-Smoked Bacon, 67
   Risotto with White Truffles, 185
   Savory Aeignets, 127
   Stuffed Potatoes, 74
   Terrine of Veal, 11
Bailey's Irish Cream
   Custard, 107
   Vanilla Ice Cream, 108
Bain-marie, 29
Banana Mousse Pie, 112
   Fruit Soup, 148
Basil, 82
   Torta Basil, 32
   Veal Chops with Sun-Dried Tomatoes and Fontina Cheese, 93
Beans: Black Bean and Madeira Soup, 168
   Filet of Beef with Oriental Black Beans and Sweet Peppers, 63
   Smoked Tuna with White Beans, 101
Beef: Beef-Veal Stock, 203
   Calves' Liver with Root Vegetables, 65
   Carpaccio (raw filet of beef), 113
      variations, 114
   Filet of Beef with Oriental Black Beans and Sweet Peppers, 63
   Glace de Viande, 204
   Shell Steak with Three Peppers, 86
   Standing Rib Roast, 124

Beef (cont.)
  Steak Putanesca, 140
  Steak Tartare, 87
Beignets, 126
  Cream Puffs, 128
  Savory Beignets, 126
  Sweet Beignets, 128
Belgian Carrots in Rosemary Butter, 91
Beurre Blanc, 122, 209
  Filet of Sole with Steamed Spinach and, 149
  Soft-Shell crabs in, with Swirls of Caviar, 164
Bisques: Lobster Bisque, 12
  Scallop Bisque with Seafood Sausage, 182
Black Beans: Filet of Beef with Sweet Peppers and, 63
  and Madeira Soup, 168
Bouillabaisse, 41, 54
  Broth, 55
  fish and shellfish, 56
  rouille, 54, 57
Bouquet garni, 191
Braised Cabbage, 169
Braised Loin of Pork with Cranberries, Sage, and Tangerines, 151
Bread: cubes for Lobster Toast, 191
  Garlic Croûtons, 218
Brie Italienne, 103
  variations, 104
Brioches: Chaud-Froid Brioches, 139
  Coulibiac, 194
  Dough, 211
Butter, 82
  Belgian Carrots in Rosemary Butter, 91
  Beurre Blanc, 209
  Chicken with Butter and Tarragon under the Skin, 8
  compound butters, 186
  lobster, 183
Butter Cream Cake, 70, 148
Butter Cream Icing, 71

Cabbage: Braised Cabbage, 169
  Corn Relish, 163
Cakes and cookies: Banana Mousse Pie, 112
  Butter Cream Cake, 70
  Lace Tulip Cookies, 189
  Odile Chocolate Cake, 100
  (See also Frostings and icings)
Calves' Liver with Root Vegetables, 65
Capelli d'Angeli with Salmon and Caviar, 187
Capons, with foie gras and truffles under the skin, 8

Carpaccio (raw filet of beef), 113
  variations, 114
Carrots: Belgian Carrots in Rosemary Butter, 91
  Calves' Liver with Root Vegetables, 65
  Chicken Pot Pie, 165
  Chicken with Butter and Tarragon under the Skin with Leeks and, 8
  glazed, 9
  Pork Curry with Root Vegetables, 89
Casseroles: Braised Loin of Pork with Cranberries, Sage and Tangerines, 151
  Chicken Pot Pie, 165
  Chicken with Garlic, Sealed in a Crust, 160
  Lobster, Shrimp, Scallops, and Leeks, 34
Caviar: Capelli d'Angeli with Salmon and, 187
  Double-Baked Potato and Leek Soufflé, 30
  Risotto with White Truffles, 184
  Soft-Shell Crabs in Beurre Blanc with Swirls of, 164
  Torta, 31
Celery root knob: Calves' Liver with Root Vegetables, 65
Charcuterie Platter, 186
Chaud-Froid Brioches, 139
Cheese: Brie Italienne, 103
  variations, 104
  chèvre: Asparagus, Westphalian Ham and Pasta with Chèvre Sauce, 69
  fontina: Sparrows' Tongues (Linguine) with Avocado and Salsa, 23
  Veal Chops with Sun-Dried Tomatoes and, 93
  grana, 221
  Double-Baked Potato and Leek Soufflé, 28
  pizza toppings, 46
  Potato Salad with Garlic, Grana, and Double-Smoked Bacon, 67
  Seafood Lasagne, 36
  Herb Toast, 52
  mozzarella: Double-Baked Potato and Leek Soufflé, 28
  Egg-Roll filling, 137
  Potatoes au-Gratin, 167
  ricotta: pizza toppings, 46
  Seafood Lasagne, 36
  Risotto with White Truffles, 183
  Savory Beignets, 127
  Seafood Lasagne, 36
  Torta, 31
Cherries: Sour Cherry Compote, 150–151

Chestnuts: Chestnut Cream with Chocolate Shavings, 153
   Pheasant with compote of Pineapple Quince, Artichoke Hearts and, 192
Chicken: with Butter and Tarragon under the Skin Accompanied by Baby Carrots and Leaks, 8
   Fried in the Southern Style, 172
   with Garlic, Sealed in a Crust, 160
   Polenta with Sausage, Chicken, and Tomato Sauce, 190
   Pot Pie, 165
   roasted, 8
   Stock, 204
Chocolate: Butter Cream Icing, 72
   Chestnut Cream with Chocolate Shavings, 153
   Frozen Espresso with Chocolate Curls and Cream, 64
   melting, 48
   Mocha Cream Icing, 71
   Odile Chocolate Cake, 100
   Raspberry Fruit Tarts with, 47
   for sealing pie crust, 113
Clams: Bouillabaisse, 54
   Seafood Lasagne, 36
   Soup, 162
Coffee: Frozen Espresso with Chocolate Curls and Cream, 64
   Mocha Cream Icing, 71
Cold Pork Salad with Cucumbers and Sesame Noodles, 68
Compotes: Pineapple Quince, Artichoke Hearts, and Chestnuts, 192
   Sour Cherry Compote, 150
Condiments, 82
Confit of Duck with Sautéed Breast of Duck, 104
Corn: Relish, 163
   Sparrows' Tongues (Linguine) with Avocado and Salsa, 23
Cornbread, 214
   Stuffing, 161
Cornichons, 82
   Steak Tartare, 87
Cornmeal, Polenta, 171
Coulibiac, 194
   brioche dough, 211
   brioche glaze, 196
   filling, 195
Crabs: Seafood Lasagne, 36
   Soft-Shell Crabs in Beurre Blanc with Swirls of Caviar, 164
Cranberries, Braised Loin of Pork with Sage, Tangerines and, 151
Cream: Filets of Striped Bass with Sweet Peppers, Lime and, 27

Frozen Espresso with Chocolate Curls and Cream, 64
Salmon Mousseline, 115
   sauces, 121
Snails in Garlic Cream, 49
Cream Puffs, 128
   savory fillings, 129
   sweet fillings, 128
Crème Fraîche, 146, 218
   Filets of Sole with Cucumber, Fresh Mint and, 30
Crêpes, 213
Croûtons, garlic, 218
Crown of Shrimp, 147
Cucumbers: Cold Pork Salad with Sesame Noodles and, 68
   Filets of Sole with Crème Fraîche, Fresh Mint and, 30
   Salad, 111
   Soup, 112
Currants: Custard, 107
   Odile Chocolate Cake, 100
Curry dishes, 42
   Pork Curry with Root Vegetables, 89
   Vegetable Curry with Hot Tortilla Chips, 123
Custard, 107

Desserts: Banana Mousse Pie, 112
   Butter Cream Cake, 70
   Chaud-Froid Brioches, 139
   Chestnut Cream with Chocolate Shavings, 153
   Cream Puffs, 128
   Custard, 107
   Food Processor Ice Cream, 108
   Food Processor Sorbet, 110
   Frozen Espresso with Chocolate Curls and Cream, 64
   Fruit Soup, 148
   Lace Tulip Cookies, 189
   Maple Walnut Pie, 170
   Odile Chocolate Cake, 100
   Pink Grapefruit Sorbet, 111
   Poached Pears, 22
   Poire Sorbet, 110
   Raspberry Fruit Tarts with Chocolate, 47
   Raspberry Ice Cream, 109
   Sabayon au Poire, 102
   Sorbets, 110
   Sour Cherry Compote, 150
   Strawberry Sorbet, 110
   Sweet Beignets, 128
   Tarte Tatin, 134
   Vanilla Ice Cream, 108
Double-Baked Potato and Leek Soufflé, 28
   variations, 29

Dough: Brioche Dough, 211
  Pasta Dough, 215
  Pastry Dough, 212
  Pizza Dough, 45
Duck: Confit of Duck, 106
  Duck Livers with Sherry Wine Vinegar, 90
  Sautéed Breast of, with Confit of Duck, 91, 104

Egg-Roll Satchels, 135
  dipping sauces, 137
  fillings, 136
  wrappers, 135
Eggs: Custard, 107
  egg-wash, 221
  Sabayon au Poire, 102
  Scrambled Eggs on Gravlax, 73
Entrées: Asparagus, Westphalian Ham, and Pasta with Chèvre Sauce, 69
  Braised Loin of Pork with Cranberries, Sage, and Tangerines, 151
  Calves' Liver with Root Vegetables, 65
  Chicken Fried in Southern Style, 172
  Chicken Pot Pie, 165
  Chicken with Butter and Tarragon under the Skin Accompanied by Baby Carrots and Leeks, 8
  Chicken with Garlic, Sealed in a Crust, 160
  Cold Pork Salad with Cucumbers and Sesame Noodles, 68
  Coulibiac, 194
  Filet of Beef with Oriental Black Beans and Sweet Peppers, 63
  Filets of Sole with Cucumber, Crème Fraîche and Fresh Mint, 30
  Filets of Striped Bass with Sweet Peppers, Lime and Cream, 27
  Lobster, Shrimp, Scallops, and Leeks, 34
  Medallions of Veal with Three Mushrooms, 154
  Pan-Broiled Swordfish with Lemon-Basil Vinaigrette, 138
  Pheasant with Compote of Pineapple Quince, Artichoke Hearts, and Chestnuts, 192
  Polenta with Sausage, Chicken, and Tomato Sauce, 190
  Pork Curry with Root Vegetables, 89
  Rack of Lamb with Rosemary and Garlic, 14
  Ragout of Lobster on a mound of Lingue di Passero, 15
  Red Snapper in Red Wine Sauce, 92
  Salmon Mousseline, 115
  Sautéed Breast of Duck with Confit of Duck, 91, 140
  Seafood Sausage, 188
  Shell Steak with Three Peppers, 86
  Shoulder of Pork with Prosciutto and Green Peppercorns, 84
  Shrimp and Scallops on Linguine, 129
  Standing Rib Roast, 124
  Steak Putanesca, 140
  Steak Tartare, 87
  Stuffed Leg of Lamb, 130
  Terrine of Veal, 11
  Veal Chops with Sun-Dried Tomatoes and Fontina Cheese, 93
Extracts and flavorings, 83

Fifth Avenue Oysters, 5
Filet of Beef with Oriental Black Beans and Sweet Peppers, 63
Filet of Sole with Beurre Blanc and Steamed Spinach, 149
Filets of Sole with Cucumber, Crème Fraîche and Fresh Mint, 30
Filets of Striped Bass with Sweet Peppers, Lime and Cream, 27
Fish and shellfish: Bouillabaisse, 54
  Clam Soup, 162
  Crown of Shrimp, 147
  egg-roll fillings, 137
  Fifth Avenue Oysters, 5
  Filet of Sole with Beurre Blanc and Steamed Spinach, 149
  Filets of Sole with Cucumber, Crème Fraîche, and Fresh Mint, 30
  Filets of Striped Bass With Sweet Peppers, Lime and Cream, 27
  Fish Fumet, 202
  Fish Stock without Fish, 202
  Haricots Verts with Bay Scallops and Sherry Wine Vinegar, 137
  Lobster, Shrimp, Scallops, and Leeks, 34
  Lobster Toast, 191
  Mussel Soup, 32
  Oysters in Garlic Cream with Shallots, 185
  Pan-Broiled Swordfish with Lemon-Basil Vinaigrette, 138
  poaching, 149, 214
  Red Snapper in Aromatic Broth with Vegetables and Ginger Hollandaise, 76
  Red Snapper in Red Wine Sauce, 92
  Salmon Mousseline, 115
    Quenelles, 118
  Scallop Bisque with Seafood Sausage, 182

Seafood Lasagne, 36
Seafood Pizza, 46
Seafood Ravioli, 43
Seafood Sausage, 188
  Scallop Bisque with, 182
Shrimp and Scallops on Linguine, 129
Smoked Tuna with White Beans, 101
Snails in Garlic Cream, 49
Soft-Shell Crabs in Beurre Blanc with Swirls of Caviar, 164
Sole Mousseline, 117
Turbot in Aromatic Broth with Vegetables, 76
(*See also* under name of fish)
Foie gras, Capon with Minced Truffles and, under the Skin, 8
Food Processors, 99
  Ice Creams, 108
  Sorbets, 110
Framboise liqueur: Fruit Soup, 148
  Poached Pears, 22
  Raspberry Ice Cream, 109
  Strawberry Sorbet, 110
Frostings and icings: Butter Cream Icing, 71
  variations, 71
  Chocolate Icing, 72, 101
  Mocha Cream Frosting, 71
  Orange Cream Icing, 71
Frozen Espresso with Chocolate Curls and Cream, 64
Fruits: Braised Loin of Pork with Cranberries, Sage and Tangerines, 151
  Chaud-Froid Brioches, 139
  fillings for cream puffs, 128
  Fruit Soup, 148
  Pheasants with Compote of Pineapple Quince, Artichoke Hearts and Chestnuts, 192
  Pink Grapefruit Sorbet, 111
  Poached Pears, 22
  Poire Sorbet, 110
  Raspberry Fruit Tarts with Chocolate, 47
  Raspberry Ice Cream, 109
  Sorbets, 110–111
  Sour Cherry Compote, 150
  Strawberry Ice Cream, 109
  Strawberry Sorbet, 110
  Sweet Beignets, 128
  Tarte Tatin, 134
  Wild Rice with Apricots and Hazelnuts, 35
Garlic: aioli sauce, 208
  Chicken with Garlic, Sealed in a Crust, 160
  Croûtons, 218

Oysters in Garlic Cream with Shallots, 185
Parboiled Sautéed Potatoes, 50
Potato Salad with Garlic, Grana, and Double-Smoked Bacon, 67
Purée, 217
Rack of Lamb with Rosemary and Garlic, 14
Sausage Toasts with Garlic Cream, 173
Snails in Garlic Cream, 49
Glace de Viande, 204
Glazes: apricot preserves, 49
  carrots, 9, 91
  chocolate, 47
  egg wash, 196
  fruit tarts, 49
  Glace de Viande, 204
  leeks, 9
  red currant jelly, 47
Glossary, 221-222
Grana, 221
  Double-Baked Potato and Leek Soufflé, 28
  pizza toppings, 46
  Potato Salad with Garlic, Grana and Double-Smoked Bacon, 67
  Seafood Lasagne, 36
Grapefruit, Pink Grapefruit Sorbet, 111
Gravlax, Scrambled Eggs on, 73
Green Beans: Haricots Verts with Bay Scallops and Sherry Wine Vinegar, 137

Ham, Asparagus, Westphalian Ham and Pasta with Chèvre Sauce, 69
Hazelnuts: Hazelnut Cream Icing, 72
  Wild Rice with Apricots and, 35

Herb Toast, 51
  variations, 52
Herbs and spices, 81–82
  fresh, 82
  Parboiled Sautéed Potatoes, 50
  Savory Beignets, 127
  Stuffed Potatoes, 74
Hollandaise sauce, 207
  Red Snapper in Aromatic Broth with Vegetables and Ginger Hollandaise, 76
  Scrambled Eggs on Gravlax, 73
  Snails in Garlic Cream, 49
Hors d'Oeuvres (*See* Appetizers)

Ice Cream: Food Processor, 108
  Raspberry Ice Cream, 109
  sorbets, 110
  Strawberry Ice Cream, 109

227

Ice Cream (*cont.*)
  Strawberry Sorbet, 110
  Vanilla Ice Cream, 108
Icings (*See* Frostings and Icings)

Jalapeño peppers: Cornbread Stuffing, 161
  Potato Salad with Sweet Red Peppers and, 132
  Salsa, 205
  Savory Beignets, 127
  Sparrows' Tongues (Linguine) with Avocado and Salsa, 23

Kale and Linguiça Soup, 176

Lace Tulip Cookies, 189
Lamb: Rack of Lamb with Rosemary and Garlic, 14
  Stuffed Leg of Lamb, 130
Lasagne, Seafood, 36
Leeks: baked, 9
  Calves' Liver with Root Vegetables, 65
  Chicken with Butter and Tarragon under the Skin with Carrots and, 8
  Double-Baked Potato and Leek Soufflé, 28
  glazed, 9
  Lobster, Shrimp, Scallops and, 34
  Pork Curry with Root Vegetables, 89
  Potato and Leek Soup, 175
Lemon Butter Cream Icing, 72
Lemons, 82
Limes with Filets of Striped Bass, Sweet Peppers and Cream, 27
Linguiça and Kale Soup, 176
Linguine (Sparrows' Tongues) with Avocado and Salsa, 23
  Shrimp and Scallops on Linguine, 129
Liver: Calves' Liver with Root Vegetables, 65
  Duck Livers with Sherry Wine Vinegar, 90
Lobster: Bouillabaisse, 54
  butter, 183
  Lobster Bisque, 12
  Lobster Toast, 191
  preparing and cooking, 12–13
  purée of coral or roe, 44
  Ragoût of Lobster on a mound of Lingue di Passero, 15
  Seafood Lasagne, 36
  Seafood Ravioli, 43
  Seafood Sausage, 188
  Shrimp, Scallops, Leeks and, 34

Macadamia Nut Icing, 71
Madeira and Black Bean Soup, 168

Maple Walnut Pie, 170
Mayonnaise, 208
  Rémoulade Sauce, 205
  variations, 208
Meats, 98
  (*See also* Beef; Lamb; Veal)
Medallions of Veal with Three Mushrooms, 154
Menus, planning, 15, 19
Meringue, 219
  Chaud-Froid Brioches, 139
Mint: Filets of Sole with Cucumber, Crème Fraîche and, 30
  Fruit Soup, 148
  Snow Peas with Shallots and, 85
Mocha Butter Cream Icing, 71
Molded Dishes: Salmon Mousseline, 115
  Terrine of Veal, 11
Monte Bianco de Marone (Chestnut Cream with Chocolate Shavings), 153
Monter au Beurre, 87, 222
Mousseline, 99
  Filet of sole, 117
  Quenelles, 118
  Salmon, 115
  Scallops, 117
Mushrooms: Chicken Pot Pie, 165
  Cornbread Stuffing, 161
  Coulibiac, 194
  Double-Baked Potato and Leek Soufflé, 29
  Medallions of Veal with Three Mushrooms, 154
  reconstituting dried, 21
  Red Snapper in Aromatic Broth, 76
  Red Snapper in Red Wine Sauce, 92
  Risotto with, 184
  Seafood Ravioli, 43
  Virginia Oak Mushrooms with Shallots, 26
  Wild Mushroom Soup, 21
Mussels: Bouillabaisse, 54
  Risotto with, 184
  Seafood Lasagne, 36
  Soup, 32

Noodles, oriental buckwheat
  Cold Pork Salad with Cucumbers and, 68
  Filet of Beef with Oriental Black Beans and Sweet Peppers, 63
Nuts: Butter Cream Icing, 71
  Hazelnut Cream Icing, 72
  Macadamia Nut Icing, 71
  Maple Walnut Pie, 170
  Wild Rice with Apricots with Hazelnuts, 35

Odile Chocolate Cake, 100
  icing, 101
Oranges: Asparagus Maltaise, 6
  Butter Cream Icing, 71
  Fruit Soup, 148
Oriental cuisine: Asparagus, Westphalian Ham, and Pasta with Chèvre Sauce, 69
  Cold Pork Salad with Cucumbers and Sesame Noodles, 68–69
  Egg-Roll Satchels, 135
  Filet of Beef with Oriental Black Beans and Sweet Peppers, 63
  Red Snapper in Aromatic Broth with Vegetables and Ginger Hollandaise, 76
Oysters: Fifth Avenue Oysters, 5
  in Garlic Cream with Shallots, 185
  Seafood Lasagne, 36
  and spinach on French bread, 104

Pan-Broiled Swordfish with Lemon-Basil Vinaigrette, 138
Parboiled Sautéed Potatoes, 50
Pasta, 41–42
  Asparagus, Westphalian Ham, and Pasta with Chèvre Sauce, 69
  Capelli d'Angeli with Salmon and Caviar, 187
  Fresh Pasta, 215
  Putanesca Sauce, 164
  Ragoût of Lobster on Mound of Lingue di Passero, 15
  Seafood Lasagne, 36
  Seafood Ravioli, 43
  Shrimp and Scallops on Linguine, 129
  Sparrows' Tongues (Linguine) with Avocado and Salsa, 23
Pastry and pies: Banana Mousse Pie, 112
  Chicken Pot Pie, 165
  Chicken with Garlic, Sealed in Crust, 160
  Maple Walnut Pie, 170
  Pastry Dough, 212
  Raspberry Fruit tarts with Chocolate, 47
  variations, 48
  sealing with apricot glaze, 48, 112
  sealing with chocolate, 113
  tart shells, 47
  Tarte Tatin, 134
Pâtés: Charcuterie Platter, 186
  Terrine of Veal, 11
Peach tarts, 48
Pears: Poached Pears, 22
  Poire Sorbet, 110
  Tarte Tatin, 134

Peppercorns: Shell Steak with Three Peppers, 86
  Shoulder of Pork with Prosciutto and Green Peppercorns, 84
Peppers: Corn Relish, 163
  Double-Baked Potato and Leek Soufflé, 30
  Filet of Beef with Oriental Black Beans and Sweet Peppers, 63
  Filets of Striped Bass with Sweet Peppers, Lime, and Cream, 27
  Potato Salad with Jalapeños and Sweet Red Peppers, 130
  Sparrows' Tongues (Linguine) with Avocado and Salsa, 23
  (*See also* Jalapeño peppers)
Pesto sauce, 98
Pheasant with a Compote of Pineapple Quince, Artichoke Hearts, and Chestnuts, 192
Pignoli nuts, 98
  Torta Basil, 32
Pineapple quince
  Pheasant with Compote of Artichoke Hearts, Chestnuts and, 192
Pink Grapefruit Sorbet, 111
Pizza: Crust, 45
  Seafood Pizza, 46
  toppings, 46
  Turnovers, 53
  White Pizza, 46
Poached Pears, 22
Poaching, 214
Poire liqueur: Sabayon au Poire, 102
Poire Sorbet, 110
Polenta, 171
  with Sausage, Chicken, and Tomato Sauce, 190
Pork: Asparagus, Westphalian Ham, and Pasta with Chèvre Sauce, 69
  Braised Loin, with Cranberries, Sage, and Tangerines, 151
  Cold Pork Salad with Cucumbers and Sesame Noodles, 68
  Curry with Root Vegetables, 89–90
  roast, 146
  Shoulder of, with Prosciutto and Green Peppercorns, 84
Potatoes, 98
  au-Gratin, 167
  Double-Baked Potato and Leek Soufflé, 28
  and Leek Soup, 175
  Linguiça and Kale Soup, 176
  Parboiled Sautéed Potatoes, 50
  pizza toppings, 46
  Salad with Garlic, Grana, and Double-Smoked Bacon, 67

229

Potatoes (*cont.*)
  Salad with Jalapeños and Sweet Red Peppers, 132
  Stuffed, 74
Poultry: Duck Livers with Sherry Wine Vinegar, 90
  (*See also* Chicken)
Prosciutto: Double-Baked Potato and Leek Soufflé, 30
  Potatoes au-Gratin, 167
  Shoulder of Pork with Green Peppercorns and, 84
Putanesca Sauce, 164

Quenelles, 118
Quince: Pheasant with Compote of Pineapple Quince, Artichoke Hearts and Chestnuts, 192

Rack of Lamb with Rosemary and Garlic, 14
Ragoûts: Artichoke, 7
  Lobster on Mound of Lingue di Passero, 15
Raspberries: Fruit Soup, 148
  Fruit Tarts with Chocolate, 47
    variations, 48
  Ice Cream, 109
  Poached Pears and, 22
Ravioli, Seafood, 43
Red Snappers: Bouillabaisse, 54
  in Aromatic Broth with Vegetables and Ginger Hollandaise, 76
  In Red Wine Sauce, 92
Relishes, Corn, 163
Remoulade Sauce, 205
Rice: Risotto with White Truffles, 183
  Wild Rice (*See* Wild Rice)
Risotto with White Truffles, 183
  variations, 184
Rosemary, 82
  Belgian Carrots in Rosemary Butter, 91
  Chicken with Butter and Rosemary under the Skin, 8
  Rack of Lamb with Rosemary and Garlic, 14

Sabayon au Poire, 102
Sage, 82
  Braised Loin of Pork with Cranberries, Sage, and Tangerines, 151
Salads: Artichoke Ragoût, 7
  Cold Pork Salad with Cucumbers and Sesame Noodles, 68
  Cucumber, 111
  Potato Salad with Garlic, Grana, and Double-Smoked Bacon, 67
  Potato Salad with Jalapeños and Sweet Red Peppers, 132

Smoked Tuna with White Beans, 101
  Wild Rice Salad, 72
Salmon: Capelli d'Angeli with Salmon and Caviar, 187
  Coulibiac, 194
  Double-Baked Potato and Leek Soufflé, 29
  Mousseline, 115
  Quenelles, 118
  Risotto with, 184
  Savory Beignets, 127
  Scrambled Eggs on Gravlax, 73
  Torta, 31
Salsa, 205
Sparrows' Tongues (Linguine) with Avocado and, 23
Salt, importance of, 81
Sauces: Asparagus, Westphalian Ham, and Pasta with Chèvre Sauce, 69
  Beurre Blanc, 209
  Braised Loin of Pork with Cranberries, Sage and Tangerines, 151
  Calves' Liver with Root Vegetables, 65
  Chicken Pot Pie, 165
  Chicken with Butter and Tarragon under the Skin, 8
  cream, 121
  Crème Fraîche, 218
  Egg-Roll Satchels, 135
  Fifth Avenue Oysters, 5
  Filets of Sole with Cucumber, Crème Fraîche, and Fresh Mint, 30
  Garlic Cream, Snails in, 49
  Haricots Verts with Bay Scallops and Sherry Wine Vinegar, 137
  hollandaise, 207
    ginger, 76
    orange, 6
  Lemon-Basil Vinaigrette, 138
  Lobster Toast, 191
  Medallions of Veal with Three Mushrooms, 154
  Pan-Broiled Swordfish with Lemon-Basil Vinaigrette, 138
  Pasta, 42
  Pheasant with Compote of Pineapple Quince, Artichoke Hearts, and Chestnuts, 192
  Pork Curry with Root Vegetables, 89
  Putanesca Sauce, 164
  Rack of Lamb with Rosemary and Garlic, 14
  Red Snapper in Red Wine Sauce, 92
  Rémoulade Sauce, 205
  Salsa, 205
  Sausage Toasts with Garlic Cream, 173
  Sautéed Breast of Duck, 91, 104

Sauces (cont.)
　Shell Steak with Three Peppers, 86
　Steak Putanesca, 140
　Steak Tartare, 87
　Tomato Sauce, 210
　Velouté, 206
Sausages: egg-roll fillings, 137
　Linguiça and Kale Soup, 176
　Pizza Turnovers, 53
　Polenta, 171
　　with Sausage, Chicken and Tomato Sauce, 190
　Potato Salad with Garlic, Grana and, 67
　Seafood Sausage, 188
　　Scallop Bisque with, 182
　Toasts with Garlic Cream, 173
Scallops: Haricots Verts with Bay Scallops and Sherry Wine Vinegar, 137
　Lobster, Shrimp, Leeks and, 34
　Mousseline of, 117
　Savory Beignets, 127
　Scallop Bisque with Seafood Sausage, 182
　Seafood Ravioli, 43
　Seafood Sausage, 188
　Shrimp and Scallops on Linguine, 129
Scrambled Eggs on Gravlax, 73
Seafood (see Fish and Shellfish)
Seafood Lasagne, 36
Seafood Pizza, 46
Seafood Ravioli, 43
Seafood Sausage, 188
　Scallop Bisque and, 182–183
Seaweed (reconstituted Japanese Hijiki), 12
　Red Snapper in Aromatic Broth with Vegetables, Ginger Hollandaise, 76
Shallots: Oysters in Garlic Cream with, 185
　Snow Peas with Fresh Mint and, 85
　Virginia Oak Mushrooms with, 26
Shell Steak with Three Peppers, 86
Sherry Wine Vinegar: Duck Livers with, 90
　Haricots Verts with Bay Scallops and, 137
　Sautéed Breast of Duck with Confit of Duck, 104
Shoulder of Pork with Prosciutto and Green Peppercorns, 84
Shrimp: Bouillabaisse, 54
　Crown of Shrimp, 147
　Double-Baked Potato and Leek Soufflé, 30
　Lobster, Scallops, Leeks and, 34
　Savory Beignets, 127

Seafood Lasagne, 36
Seafood Ravioli, 43
Seafood Sausage, 188
Shrimp and Scallops on Linguine, 129
Smoked Tuna with White Beans, 101
Snails in Garlic Cream, 49
Snow peas: Chicken Pot Pie, 165
　Filet of Beef with Oriental Black Beans and Sweet Peppers, 63
　with Fresh Mint and Shallots, 85
　Red Snapper in Aromatic Broth with Vegetables and Ginger Hollandaise, 76
Soft-Shell Crabs in Beurre Blanc with Swirls of Caviar, 164
Sole, filet of: with Beurre Blanc and Steamed Spinach, 149
　Mousseline of, 117
　Seafood Ravioli, 43
　Seafood Sausage, 188
Sorbets, 110
　Pink Grapefruit Sorbet, 111
　Strawberry Sorbet, 110
Soufflés, Double-Baked Potato and Leek, 28
Soups and stocks: Beef-Veal Stock, 203
　Black Bean and Madeira Soup, 168
　Bouillabaisse, 54
　Chicken Stock, 204
　Clam Soup, 162
　court bouillon, 182
　Cucumber Soup, 112
　duck stock, 105
　Fish Fumet, 202
　Fish Stock without Fish, 202
　Fruit Soup, 148
　Linguiça and Kale Soup, 176
　Lobster Bisque, 12
　Mussel Soup, 32
　Potato and Leek Soup, 175
　Red Snapper in an Aromatic Broth, 76
　Scallop Bisque with Seafood Sausage, 182
　Spinach Soup, 10
　Wild Mushroom Soup, 21
Sour Cherry Compote, 150
Sparrows' Tongues (Linguine) with Avocado and Salsa, 23
Spinach: Baked Spinach, 125
　Filet of Sole with Beurre Blanc and Steamed, 149
　and oysters on French bread, 104
　Spinach Soup, 10
　Steamed Spinach, 216
　Stuffed Leg of Lamb, 131
Standing Rib Roast, 124
Steak Putanesca, 140

231

Steak Tartare, 87
   Served on slices of French bread, 104
Stocks (see Soups and stocks)
Strawberries: Fruit Soup, 148
   Ice Cream, 109
   Sorbet, 110
String beans: Haricots Verts with Bay Scallops and Sherry Wine Vinegar, 137
Striped Bass: Bouillabaisse, 54
   Filets with Sweet Peppers, Lime and Cream, 27
   poaching, 27
Stuffed Leg of Lamb, 131
Stuffed Potatoes, 74
Stuffings; Braised Loin of Pork with Cranberries, Sage, and Tangerines, 151
   Cornbread Stuffing, 161
Sugar, 83
Swordfish, Pan-Broiled with Lemon-Basil Vinaigrette, 138

Tangerines, Braised Loin of Pork with Cranberries, Sage and, 151
Tarragon, 82
   Chicken with Butter and Tarragon under the Skin, 8
Tart shells, 47
   sealing the crust, 48
Tarte Tatin, 134
Terrine of Veal, 11
Tomatoes: egg-roll fillings, 137
   Fifth Avenue Oysters, 5
   Herb Toast, 82
   pizza toppings, 46
   Salsa, 205
   Tomato Sauce, 210
      Polenta with Sausage, Chicken and, 190
   Veal Chops with Sun-Dried Tomatoes and Fontina Cheese, 93
Torta, 31
Tortilla chips: Sparrows' Tongues (Linguine) with Avocado and Salsa, 23
   Vegetable Curry with, 123
Truffles: Capon with Foie Gras and Minced Truffles under the Skin, 8
   Risotto with White Truffles, 183
   Torta with Black Truffles, 32
Tuna fish: Putanesca Sauce, 164
   Smoked Tuna with White Beans, 101
Turbot in Aromatic Broth with Vegetables and Ginger Hollandaise, 76
Turnips en Papillote, 133

Vanilla Ice Cream, 108
Veal: Beef-Veal Stock, 203
   Chops with Sun-Dried Tomatoes and Fontina Cheese, 93
   Medallions of, with Three Mushrooms, 154
   Terrine of Veal, 11
Vegetables: Artichoke Ragoût, 7
   Baked Spinach, 125
   Belgian Carrots in Rosemary Butter, 91
   Braised Cabbage, 169
   Calves' Liver with Root Vegetables, 65
   Cucumber Salad, 111
   Curry with Hot Tortilla Chips, 123
   Double-Baked Potato and Leek Soufflé, 28
   egg-roll filling, 137
   Haricots Verts with Bay Scallops and Sherry Vine Vinegar, 137
   Linguica and Kale Soup, 176
   Parboiled Sautéed Potatoes, 50
   Pork Curry with Root Vegetables, 89
   Potato and Leek Soup, 175
   Potato Salad with Garlic, Grana, and Double-Smoked Bacon, 67
   Potatoes, Stuffed, 74
   Potatoes au-Gratin, 167
   Red Snapper in Aromatic Broth with Vegetables and Ginger Hollandaise, 76
   Snow Peas with Fresh Mint and Shallots, 85
   Spinach, Baked, 125
   Terrine of Veal, 11
   Turnips en Papillote, 133
   Vegetable Curry with Hot Tortilla Chips, 123
   (See also under name of vegetable)
Velouté, 206
Coulibiac, 194
Vinegar, 82
   Pan-Broiled Swordfish with Lemon-Basil Vinaigrette, 138
   Sherry Wine, 83
      Duck Livers with, 90
      Haricots Verts with Bay Scallops and, 137
      Sautéed Breast of Duck with Confit of Duck, 104
Virginia Oak Mushrooms with Shallots, 26

Walnuts: Maple Walnut Pie, 170
Westphalian Ham, Asparagus, Pasta with Chèvre Sauce, 69
Wild Mushroom Soup, 21
Wild Rice, 215
   with Apricots and Hazelnuts, 35, 91
   Salads, 72–73

About the Author

Earle Sieveling was one of the better-known dancers with George Balanchine's New York City Ballet, partnering such greats as Maria Tallchief, Violette Verdy, Suzanne Farrell, and a myriad of others.

While he had always had an interest in fine food, his touring with the company all over the world helped him produce a unique attitude toward food as both an art form and part of the love of life.

After Sieveling retired from City Ballet he began a new career as a professional chef, founding Sperry's Café and The Dacha during the summer seasons at Saratoga Springs, New York, and Odile in New York City. It was during these years that he originated *New York Cuisine*. He has also been instrumental in the development of Soho Charcuterie and Capsouto Frères. "Stendahl on Food" declared his Odile chocolate cake "New York's perfect chocolate cake." His prepared foods are featured at Dean & DeLuca, New York and East Hampton.

In addition to his other activities he is one of the founders of a fine-food marketing and advertising consulting firm.

To "Miss Ann," whose brilliance shone in this book as its guiding light from germination to full flower. How can I thank you. . . ?